PING
WOMEN'S GOLF YEAR

second
EDITION

· EDITED BY NICK EDMUND ·

WITH A
FOREWORD BY
JOANNE CARNER

IN ASSOCIATION WITH
WEETABIX

KENSINGTON WEST
PRODUCTIONS

First published 1994

© Nick Edmund 1994

Nick Edmund has asserted his right under
the Copyright, Designs and Patents Act, 1988
to be identified as the author of this work

First published in the United Kingdom in 1994 by
Kensington West Productions

A CIP catalogue record for this book is available
from the British Library
ISBN 1 871349 27 3

Designed by Rob Kelland at Allsport
Typeset in Perpetua and Twentieth Century
Colour reproduction by Trinity Graphic, Hong Kong
Printed and bound in Italy by New Interlitho S.p.A.

PING ® is a registered Trade Mark of
Karsten Manufacturing Corporation

PHOTOGRAPHIC CREDITS

Allsport: 6, 48 (right), 49 (top), 72, 94 (both), 100, 126, 136, 142, 146, 153, 154, 155;
Claus Anderson/Allsport USA: 56; **David Cannon/Allsport:** 12 (right), 13 (top), 20-21,
28 (right), 32, 33, 34 (left), 35, 67 (left), 75, 86-87, 112, 120, 129 (inset), 130, 150, 151, 157;
Stephen Dunn/Allsport USA: 23, 28 (left), 64 (right), 67 (right), 82, 93 (left), 128, 133, 134;
Stephen Munday/Allsport: 16, 44-45, 47 (right), 49 (below), 50 (all), 51 (both), 90 (left), 91, 97, 101,
105, 110-111, 117, 123, 131, 140-141, 147; **Gary Newkirk/Allsport USA:** 11 (below), 14, 36-37, 38, 39
(both), 40, 41, 42 (both), 43, 73 (right) 126 (inset), 135 (right); **Rick Stewart/Allsport USA:** 17 (left), 57;
Michael C. Cohen: 29; **Bob Ewell:** 5, 8-9, 10, 13 (below), 15 (top), 18, 19, 24-25, 26, 27 (right), 52-53,
54, 55 (both), 58-59, 61, 64 (left), 65, 70, 73 (left), 74, 77, 93 (right), 103, 115, 122, 137, 158;
The Greenbrier: 129, 148-149, 159; **Rob Griffin:** 4, 15 (below); **Matthew Harris:** 47 (left);
Gary Kobayashi: 114,116; **Laing the Jeweller:** 107; **Steve Murphy:** 68;
Eric Hepworth: 89, 92, 95, 128 (inset); **Debbie Newcombe:** 99, 106 (right), 144;
Mark Newcombe: 11 (top), 12 (left), 17 (right), 27 (left), 30-31, 34 (right), 46, 48 (left), 62-63 (all),
66, 69, 81, 83, 90 (right), 98, 106 (left), 109, 113, 118-119, 124, 127, 135 (main), 152, 156;
Royal Golf Club, Evian: 125; **Robert Walker/USGA:** 85, 143

Contents

All text by Nick Edmund unless otherwise credited

A Welcome

From Karsten and Louise Solheim

We will remember the golf year 1993 as the year Patty Sheehan walked into the LPGA Hall of Fame in our own 'backyard'. Her thrilling victory in the Standard Register Ping tournament at Moon Valley, making her only the 13th Hall of Fame member, was clearly the highlight of the year in women's golf.

It was a year that saw the continued emergence in the United States of a group of European players fresh off their Solheim Cup victory in Dalmahoy, Scotland. We watched with pride as Arizona native Lauri Merten charged to victory at the US Women's Open – signalling her return to the form she exhibited so early in her career. And, sadly, it was a year we said good-bye to another Arizonan so close to our hearts – Heather Farr.

All of which (and much more) you will see detailed in the following pages. Editor Nick Edmund has again compiled a stellar list of contributing writers and photographers to bring you a comprehensive look at the world of women's golf.

We extend our thanks to 1994 US Solheim Cup captain JoAnne Carner for contributing the foreword. The tenacity she exhibited in match-play golf will surely serve her team well as they face a very confident European side that is again captained by Mickey Walker. We look forward to a hard-fought match at The Greenbrier in late October.

Until then, we'll watch with much enthusiasm as another year unfolds.

Enjoy the book.

KARSTEN AND LOUISE SOLHEIM

Foreword

By JoAnne Carner

This is a very special time for me. To be Captain of the United States Solheim Cup team is not only a great honor but will, I'm sure, prove to be one of the biggest thrills of my career.

As many of you may recall, I played in several Curtis Cup matches as an amateur and I believe there is nothing more exciting than the head-to-head, cut and thrust nature of matchplay competition. To be playing for your country, or representing your continent increases the pleasure (and pressure!) one hundred percent.

It can be great fun too and when you win you feel really euphoric; mind you, when you lose you feel as if you've let your whole team down. The thrill of the battle, that's what it's all about and that's what I want to impart to my team.

The Solheim Cup is to be staged at The Greenbrier, West Virginia, which many regard as the finest hotel and golf complex in America. I don't think the design of the course will favor one side or the other but with the match being held in October, with all the leaves turning color, the setting will be stunning and it's an occasion that no one wants to miss.

Since Europe's victory at Dalmahoy, interest in the Solheim Cup seems to have become equally strong on both sides of the Atlantic and it is surely good for golf that the women's game can now boast a truly international array of stars and personalities.

This colorful second edition of the Ping Women's Golf Year captures this international flavor, plus all the excitement – the many moments of glory and despair – from 1993 and sets the scene perfectly for 1994. I'm sure it's going to be a tremendous season and I'm sure you will enjoy every page of this book.

JoAnne Carner

Introduction

By Nick Edmund

Greetings. Welcome to this 2nd edition of the *Ping Women's Golf Year*. If you are not familiar with the 1st edition we hope that your initial reaction on seeing the publication is something along the lines of... 'At long last... a detailed, full colour, annual review of women's golf!' For how many attractively produced, coffee table-type books are there that exist to celebrate the unique colour and excitement of the women's game – both amateur and professional?

And if you agree that it is attractively produced, then the first people we must thank are our generous sponsors: firstly, Karsten Manufacturing Corporation, the Phoenix-based creators of Ping golf equipment, and secondly, Weetabix, title sponsors to Europe's most prestigious women's golf tournament, the Weetabix British Open. Without their support and encouragement this project could never have succeeded.

The 2nd edition of the *Ping Women's Golf Year* surveys the world of women's golf as season 1993 passes into season 1994. The book has eight chapters, in which are detailed the achievements of the best women players as they embark on the year's important tournaments and matches. The destiny of the Major championships and the golf seasons in Europe and America are explored in detail. Golf in 'the rest of the world' is not forgotten and the final three chapters preview the big events of 1994 including, of course, the Solheim Cup at The Greenbrier and the Curtis Cup at The Honors Course, Chattanooga.

Having thanked our sponsors, as editor I would next like to thank our publishers, Kensington West Productions and, of course, JoAnne Carner for providing the foreword. As the 1st edition contained a foreword by Mickey Walker no one can accuse this publication of bias! With this in mind may I wish both Captains the best of British luck for their match in October.

We are fortunate to have assembled such an impressive international collection of contributing journalists and photographers. The book is beautifully illustrated and I would especially like to thank David Cannon, Mark Newcombe and Bob Ewell (the book's principal photographers) for their outstanding contributions and advice.

The finished product would not be half as attractive either without the considerable input of designer, Rob Kelland, and nor could it have been produced in the time it was without the support of the leading sports picture agency, Allsport, who kindly allowed the book to be put together on their premises; from super-fast typist Julie Kay to UK Managing Director, Adrian Murrell, I am extremely grateful to them.

NICK EDMUND

1993
A Memorable Season

1993
A Memorable Season

An Overview

Memorable? It was certainly that. 1993 was a year full of landmarks and firsts, a season of surprises and a season of ultimate triumph – or last-gasp glory. It was a momentous year for four Americans. Patty Sheehan gained her 30th Tour victory, so securing admission to the

A legend and a future legend? Nancy Lopez and Brandie Burton

LPGA Hall of Fame – and a very special place in golf history. 21 year-old Brandie Burton became the youngest ever winner of a Major championship and Lauri Merten, without a win of any kind in nine years, captured the US Women's Open with a birdie at the 72nd hole. Each of these events happened on American soil, but the LPGA Tour staged its final tournament of the year in Japan, and with her final putt on the final green Betsy King scooped all the major end-of-season awards. Now *she* stands on the threshold of the Hall of Fame.

Rarely does a year go by without Britain's Laura Davies making a significant impact on both sides of the Atlantic. But in 1993 she also made an impression on the distant fringes of the Pacific. Davies was the only player – male or female – who recorded victories on four continents. As well as being spread across the globe, her wins were neatly spaced on the calendar. In January she won an event on the Asian Circuit in Thailand and in May added the McDonald's Championship to her growing collection of LPGA titles. Back on home soil in September, Davies retained the English Open at Tytherington and then finally in December – not too many days before Christmas and 12,000 miles from Tytherington – she won the Australian Masters – her 25th professional victory.

Then there were the memorable performances of the mighty Swedes, Helen

(Left) Laura Davies won four tournaments on four continents in 1993. (Below) US Open champion, Lauri Merten parades the greatest prize in women's golf

Alfredsson and Annika Sorenstam. The Swedish are said to be an unemotional race... in which case meet two exceptions to the rule. In the 'Overview' to the first edition of this book we charted Alfredsson's meteoric rise to prominence and, after detailing her considerable achievements in 1992, we asked 'How do you follow a season like that?' She produced the perfect answer by becoming the first European winner of the year's first Major, the Nabisco Dinah Shore tournament at Mission Hills. Unemotional? Check with her playing partner that day, Betsy King. Alfredsson went on to finish fifth on the 1993 LPGA Money List, yet surprisingly was unable to win in Europe (although to be fair, she didn't play in very many European events).

Enter 'Annika the Great'. The golfing world had been eagerly awaiting the start of Annika Sorenstam's professional career after her spectacular successes as an amateur. For

two years Sorenstam had vied with America's Vicki Goetze for recognition as the unofficial 'world's leading amateur'. In September 1992 she collected the Leading Individual prize at the World Amateur Team Championships in Vancouver, winning by five shots. As a Swede, she was of course ineligible for the Curtis Cup, but while we couldn't watch her at Hoylake in 1992, so successful was she in her first professional season that it seems likely we will see her at The Greenbrier in October 1994. If the present trend continues, the official language for the European Solheim Cup team could soon switch to Swedish.

Sorenstam's remarkable rookie season made her our choice as 'European Golfer of the Year' and she is profiled by Patricia Davies in Chapter Four. (Patty Sheehan, our 'American Golfer of the Year' is profiled by Sonja Steptoe in Chapter Three).

Helen Alfredsson's victory in the Dinah Shore came just seven days after Patty Sheehan marched triumphantly into the Hall of Fame at Moon Valley. Alfredsson's victory appeared to trigger an amazing run

(Right) Helen Alfredsson won the Dinah Shore tournament in March and nearly captured the US Open crown in July,
(left) Karen Lunn, winner of the Weetabix British Open and the European Order of Merit

of success for the elite band of Europeans playing on the LPGA Tour. Trish Johnson, who won successive tournaments, Laura Davies and 'Alfie' herself, spent much of the American Spring and early Summer perched near the top of the LPGA Money List. No doubt it was purely coincidental, but the European tide seemed capable of being stemmed only when Patty Sheehan was back on the winners rostrum. Patty certainly picked the right occasion to rediscover her winning ways, for her career-win number 31 was the LPGA Championship, which she captured in June at Bethesda in Maryland. Should that win constitute 'Major title number four' for Sheehan, or 'Major title number five', depends on whether the British Open is regarded as a bona fide Major. Either way, it was Sheehan who was ready and present to defend both championships in 1993 – the US Women's Open at Crooked Stick and the Weetabix British Open at Woburn.

To say that these two great championships produced different outcomes

(Above) Patty Sheehan wins her third LPGA Championship at Bethesda. (Right) After the deluge: mopping up at the du Maurier Classic

1993 was the year
when Ayako Okamoto
finally won the
Japanese
National Open

Ping Women's Golf Year

would be an enormous understatement. On the eve of the final round of the US Open there were still several players who maintained realistic chances of winning. Playing just as superbly as she had at Mission Hills, Helen Alfredsson led by two strokes after 54 holes. But looking at the star-studded leaderboard on Saturday evening it was as if the Americans had brought out all their 'heavy artillery' to prevent Alfredsson (or Japanese challenger Hiromi Kobayashi) from taking the title out of the country.

Patty Sheehan, Pat Bradley, Nancy Lopez and Donna Andrews were all poised to challenge on the final day but it still looked as if Alfredsson might complete an amazing Dinah Shore – US Open double... until Lauri Merten appeared on the scene. Over one of the toughest closing stretches in golf, Merten unleashed a magnificent birdie-par-birdie finish. The consequence was that Alfredsson now needed to birdie her final hole to force a play-off... but her 12 foot putt to tie missed by a fraction of an inch – so often the margin between glory and despair.

There wasn't a 'margin' as such at Woburn in August – more like a gulf. Australian Karen Lunn produced the greatest performance of her life to destroy a quality field. She actually won by eight strokes from Brandie Burton, with the rest of the field strung out somewhere across Buckinghamshire. Lunn went on to win the WPG European Order of Merit, but an indication as to how impressive her performance was at Woburn came just 14 days later when Burton captured the final LPGA Major of the year, the rain-interrupted du Maurier Classic, after a play-off with Betsy King.

It was at the du Maurier that King made

(Left) Could it be jet-lag? Trish Johnson divides her time between Europe and America
(Below) Rising star of the LPGA Tour, Donna Andrews

her much publicised comment that she expected Burton to win 'more tournaments than any other player during the next 10 years'. Although she only won once last year, 1992's Player of the Year, Dottie Mochrie may have something to say about that – as indeed might Donna Andrews, America, is approximately twice Burton's age, but last year she finally fulfilled a great ambition by winning the Japanese National Open, her country's most important event. In recent years Okamoto has had to look increasingly over her shoulder at the new faces who now appear ready to challenge her

Annika Sorenstam played in nine events in Europe and finished second on four occasions Michelle McGann and a few more of the LPGA Tour's leading young players.

It is still hard to believe that Burton is only 21 – or at least was that age when she won her first Major title last summer, or that she has already amassed career earnings in excess of $1 million.

Ayako Okamoto, a player who is idolised in Japan even more than Nancy Lopez is in position as Japanese number one. Pat Bradley, Beth Daniel and Betsy King will know how she feels.

The struggle for dominance between the young and the not-so-young wasn't a significant issue on the LPGA Tour last year, as it had been in 1992. For the first half of the season the so-called 'European invasion' regularly grabbed the headlines; later the preoccupation seemed to be, 'when will Betsy win?' It was easy to lose count of the number of times that King went into the final round of a tournament leading or in a share of the lead, only to falter on the final day. At least (and with perfect theatrical timing) it all came right in the end.

In Europe if there were any 'invaders', they were Australians led by Karen Lunn;

Lorenzi added the 'last-gasp victory'.

Later this year ten Europeans will travel to America and attempt to retain the Solheim Cup. They will confront an

Brandie Burton (below left) wins her first Major; according to Betsy King (below) she has the potential to dominate women's golf in the '90s

but 1993 clearly belonged to Annika Sorenstam and to the trio of young first-time winners: Helen Dobson, Lora Fairclough and Amaya Arruti. Between them they provided the 'firsts' and the 'shocks'; as always it was Laura (25 victories) Davies who provided the 'landmark' achievement; Helen Alfredsson secured the 'ultimate triumph' and France's Marie-Laure de

inspired, determined and multi-talented team led by JoAnne Carner. Come October, Betsy King will surely have secured her place alongside Patty Sheehan and Nancy Lopez in the LPGA Hall of Fame. Brandie Burton, Dottie Mochrie and Donna Andrews will be fired up as never before. Is there any hope for Europe? Of course: ask Laura Davies. And ask those emotional Swedes.

World Rankings:
The Ping Leaderboard

AS OF 31 DECEMBER 1993

POSITION		POINTS TOTAL
1	Patty Sheehan (US)	256.28
2	Betsy King (US)	240.48
3	Brandie Burton (US)	231.65
4	Dottie Mochrie (US)	222.30
5	Laura Davies (England)	195.13
6	Helen Alfredsson (Sweden)	179.55
7	Nancy Lopez (US)	134.18
8	Meg Mallon (US)	134.00
9	Trish Johnson (England)	133.93
10	Tammie Green (US)	123.73
11	Donna Andrews (US)	116.83
12	Ayako Okamoto (Japan)	115.60
13	Jane Geddes (US)	111.05
14	Danielle Ammaccapane (US)	109.50
15	Sherri Steinhauer (US)	109.47
16	Juli Inkster (US)	106.45
17	Dawn Coe-Jones (Canada)	104.05
18	Lauri Merten (US)	103.30
19	Hiromi Kobayashi (Japan)	99.01
20	Mayumi Hirase (Japan)	94.60
21	Rosie Jones (US)	93.20
22	Dana Lofland (US)	90.00
23	Michelle McGann (US)	89.78
24	Liselotte Neumann (Sweden)	86.05
25	Mayumi Murai (Japan)	82.80
26	Judy Dickinson (US)	82.37
27	Karen Lunn (Australia)	79.83
28	Deb Richard (US)	78.75
29	Tina Barrett (US)	76.45
30	Beth Daniel (US)	75.90
31	Michiko Hattori (Japan)	75.25
32	Toshimi Kimura (Japan)	73.80
33	Colleen Walker (US)	71.30
34	Kris Monaghan (US)	71.08
35	Missie Berteotti (US)	70.03
36	Alison Nicholas (England)	69.56
37	Jane Crafter (Australia)	68.90
38	Patti Rizzo (US)	67.70
39	Annika Sorenstam (Sweden)	67.65
40	Pat Bradley (US)	66.63
41	Corinne Dibnah (Australia)	65.63
42	Ai-Yu Tu (Taiwan)	65.55
43	Kristi Albers (US)	65.25
44	Hollis Stacy (US)	60.75
45	Kelly Robbins (US)	60.10
46	Kumiko Hiyoshi (Japan)	59.75
47	Amy Benz (US)	58.85
48	Florence Descampe (Belgium)	54.50
49	Cindy Rarick (US)	52.60
50	Kaori Harada (Japan)	52.30

(Right)
Liselotte Neumann;
(opposite page)
Patty Sheehan

*The Ping Leaderboard is a world-wide ranking table designed
to reflect players' performances over a rolling 24 month period

2 The Major Championships

The Major Championships

· ROLL OF HONOUR ·

NABISCO DINAH SHORE

1972	Jane Blalock
1973	Mickey Wright
1974	Jo Ann Prentice
1975	Sandra Palmer
1976	Judy Rankin
1977	Kathy Whitworth
1978	Sandra Post
1979	Sandra Post
1980	Donna Caponi
1981	Nancy Lopez
1982	Sally Little
1983*	Amy Alcott
1984	Juli Inkster
1985	Alice Miller
1986	Pat Bradley
1987	Betsy King
1988	Amy Alcott
1989	Juli Inkster
1990	Betsy King
1991	Amy Alcott
1992	Dottie Mochrie
1993	Helen Alfredsson

*Designated a Major from 1983

LPGA CHAMPIONSHIP

1955	Beverly Hanson
1956	Marlene Hagge
1957	Louise Suggs
1958	Mickey Wright
1959	Betsy Rawls
1960	Mickey Wright
1961	Mickey Wright
1962	Judy Kimball
1963	Mickey Wright
1964	Mary Mills
1965	Sandra Haynie
1966	Gloria Ehret
1967	Kathy Whitworth
1968	Sandra Post
1969	Betsy Rawls
1970	Shirley Englehorn
1971	Kathy Whitworth
1972	Kathy Ahern
1973	Mary Mills
1974	Sandra Haynie
1975	Kathy Whitworth
1976	Betty Burfeindt
1977	Chako Higuchi
1978	Nancy Lopez
1979	Donna Caponi
1980	Sally Little
1981	Donna Caponi
1982	Jan Stephenson
1983	Patty Sheehan
1984	Patty Sheehan
1985	Nancy Lopez
1986	Pat Bradley
1987	Jane Geddes
1988	Sherri Turner
1989	Nancy Lopez
1990	Beth Daniel
1991	Meg Mallon
1992	Betsy King
1993	Patty Sheehan

US WOMEN'S OPEN

1946	Patty Berg
1947	Betty Jameson
1948	Babe Zaharias
1949	Louise Suggs
1950	Babe Zaharias
1951	Betsy Rawls
1952	Louise Suggs
1953	Betsy Rawls
1954	Babe Zaharias
1955	Fay Crocker
1956	Kathy Cornelius
1957	Betsy Rawls
1958	Mickey Wright
1959	Mickey Wright
1960	Betsy Rawls
1961	Mickey Wright
1962	Murle Lindstrom
1963	Mary Mills
1964	Mickey Wright
1965	Carol Mann
1966	Sandra Spuzich
1967	Catherine Lacoste
1968	Susie Berning
1969	Donna Caponi
1970	Donna Caponi
1971	JoAnne Carner
1972	Susie Berning
1973	Susie Berning
1974	Sandra Haynie
1975	Sandra Palmer
1976	JoAnne Carner
1977	Hollis Stacy
1978	Hollis Stacy

1979	Jerilyn Britz
1980	Amy Alcott
1981	Pat Bradley
1982	Janet Alex
1983	Jan Stephenson
1984	Hollis Stacy
1985	Kathy Baker
1986	Jane Geddes
1987	Laura Davies
1988	Liselotte Neumann
1989	Betsy King
1990	Betsy King
1991	Meg Mallon
1992	Patty Sheehan
1993	Lauri Merten

WEETABIX BRITISH OPEN

1976	Jenny Lee-Smith	1985	Betsy King
1977	Vivien Saunders	1986	Laura Davies
1978	Janet Melville	1987	Alison Nicholas
1979	Alison Sheard	1988	Corinne Dibnah
1980	Debbie Massey	1989	Jane Geddes
1981	Debbie Massey	1990	Helen Alfredsson
1982	Marta Figueras-Dotti	1991	Penny Grice-Whittaker
1983	No Championship	1992	Patty Sheehan
1984	Ayako Okamoto	1993	Karen Lunn

DU MAURIER LTD. CLASSIC

1973	Jocelyne Bourassa
1974	Carole Jo Callison
1975	JoAnne Carner
1976	Donna Caponi
1977	Judy Rankin
1978	JoAnne Carner
1979*	Amy Alcott
1980	Pat Bradley
1981	Jan Stephenson
1982	Sandra Haynie
1983	Hollis Stacy
1984	Juli Inkster
1985	Pat Bradley
1986	Pat Bradley
1987	Jody Rosenthal
1988	Sally Little
1989	Tammie Green
1990	Cathy Johnston
1991	Nancy Scranton
1992	Sherri Steinhauer
1993	Brandie Burton

*Designated a Major from 1979

*Brandie Burton, 21 year-old winner
of the 1993 du Maurier Classic*

Nabisco
Dinah Shore

1993 Nabisco Dinah Shore

25 - 28 MARCH • MISSION HILLS COUNTRY CLUB, RANCHO MIRAGE, CALIFORNIA

There had, of course, been much to talk about in the run-up to the eagerly awaited first (and arguably most glamorous) Major of 1993. Victory at Mission Hills 12 months earlier had totally transformed the career of Dottie Mochrie; from being a very promising, two-time winner at the start of the year she suddenly became the player to beat and by the end of the 1992 season — during which she mounted the winners' rostrum on no fewer than four occasions — she was the tour's Leading Moneywinner and Player of the Year.

Then there was Patty Sheehan. Never mind what had begun 12 months earlier, what about the events of seven days ago! By virtue of her triumph in the Standard Register Ping tournament at Moon Valley Sheehan had collected career win number 30 thereby gaining entry into the LPGA Hall of Fame: immortality had been secured.

Helen Alfredsson was a mere spectator at the 1992 Dinah Shore (it was the beginning of her rookie season in America) yet her performances around the world in the ensuing months had certainly elevated her career to a higher plane... but surely 'Alfie' wasn't ready to win the Dinah Shore — the so-called 'Masters of women's golf'? For one thing, no European player had ever won the tournament and, secondly, the Swedish golfer had still to achieve her first victory on US soil.

Well, she got off to a terrific start. A

Thursday at dawn: great expectations for a glorious stage. The curtain was ready to rise on the 1993 major season and all the talk and attention seemed to be focused on Dottie and Patty. Yet, come late Sunday afternoon when the curtain fell, it was 'Alfie' who had stolen the show.

three under par 69 put her just a stroke behind first round leaders Nancy Lopez, Missie Berteotti and Spain's Marta Figueras-Dotti, and a second day 71 moved her into a share of the half-way lead with Figueras-Dotti, Pat Bradley and Dawn Coe-Jones. Lopez soared to a 78 on Friday (her round

fell away during the third round. The weather was nigh-on perfect but picturesque Mission Hills seemed to be playing even tougher than usual. Alfredsson and the Canadian Coe-Jones posted matching level par 72s and remained ahead of the field. Only one golfer made a significant move on

(Opposite page) Dottie Mochrie; (above) Helen Alfredsson included a two shot penalty for slow-play) while Mochrie could never recover from a disastrous opening 77 and, though still in touch after 36 holes, Sheehan would fall away after scoring a 76 on Saturday.

In fact, many of the major contenders

Saturday and it was a significant golfer who made it – Betsy King, winner of the event in 1987 and 1990 who produced the best round of the week. King fired seven birdies in the third round and her 67 lifted her in to a share of the lead at four under par.

Helped by an eagle at the 6th, Nancy Lopez scored a 68 on Thursday

Alfredsson, Coe-Jones and King: the Swede, the Canadian and the American. They played together in the final three-ball on Sunday and between them could boast a total of 29 LPGA titles — none for Alfredsson, one for Coe-Jones and 28 (including 5 Majors) for Betsy King. What

chance an upset?

A King victory seemed the most likely result, of course, especially when she immediately took the lead on Sunday with a birdie at the first. But it was to prove an extremely frustrating day for King. She didn't play particularly poorly, rather she

King's title dreams slip away as 'Alfie' (far left) steals the show

steadily frittered away shots and when Coe-Jones started to do likewise 'all' Alfredsson needed to do was reel off a succession of pars to claim an historic victory (as if par golf were ever easy under such pressure!). For much of the round she did precisely that, although two superb birdies at the 8th and 9th holes allowed her the luxury of taking six at the par five 18th.

So, in the same Spring fortnight that a German golfer won the Masters at Augusta, a Swedish golfer won the Dinah Shore at Mission Hills. Langer and Alfredsson — like chalk and cheese: one is super-cool, one is super-charged. Which is the emotional one? Eyes to the left.

Sweden's Helen Alfredsson tells the world how she won her first Major title

1993 NABISCO DINAH SHORE

25 - 28 MARCH • MISSION HILLS COUNTRY CLUB, RANCHO MIRAGE, CALIFORNIA

Player	R1	R2	R3	R4	Total	Prize	Player	R1	R2	R3	R4	Total	Prize
Helen Alfredsson	69	71	72	72	284	$105,000	Caroline Keggi	74	74	73	72	293	6,304
Amy Benz	72	73	71	70	286	49,901	Danielle Ammaccapane	69	75	74	75	293	6,304
Tina Barrett	70	73	72	71	286	49,901	Cindy Schreyer	75	70	72	76	293	6,304
Betsy King	71	74	67	74	286	49,901	Anne-Marie Palli	70	71	76	76	293	6,304
Hollis Stacy	72	74	71	70	287	25,126	Marta Figueras-Dotti	68	72	75	78	293	6,304
Missie Berteotti	68	74	73	72	287	25,126	Dana Lofland-Dormann	76	75	75	68	294	4,740
Dawn Coe-Jones	72	68	72	75	287	25,126	Dottie Mochrie	77	73	74	70	294	4,740
Nancy Lopez	68	78	72	70	288	15,762	Heather Drew	79	70	74	71	294	4,740
Brandie Burton	73	73	68	74	288	15,762	Val Skinner	73	75	74	72	294	4,740
Trish Johnson	74	68	72	74	288	15,762	Allison Finney	70	73	79	72	294	4,740
Jane Crafter	71	72	70	75	288	15,762	Cindy Rarick	76	75	70	73	294	4,740
Patty Sheehan	73	70	76	70	289	10,625	Sherri Turner	73	72	76	73	294	4,740
Debbie Massey	70	74	74	71	289	10,625	Terry-Jo Myers	74	73	73	74	294	4,740
Tammie Green	72	73	72	72	289	10,625	Joan Pitcock	70	72	76	76	294	4,740
Laura Davies	72	72	73	72	289	10,625	Sherri Steinhauer	72	74	71	77	294	4,740
Pamela Wright	74	68	75	72	289	10,625	Liselotte Neumann	72	76	75	72	295	3,173
Pat Bradley	71	69	75	74	289	10,625	JoAnne Carner	78	73	71	73	295	3,173
Kris Monaghan	76	71	74	69	290	8,806	Patti Rizzo	74	77	71	73	295	3,173
Donna Andrews	73	74	72	72	291	8,101	Juli Inkster	75	73	73	74	295	3,173
Karen Noble	74	72	70	75	291	8,101	Maggie Will	72	73	76	74	295	3,173
Nancy Scranton	73	72	71	75	291	8,101	Shelley Hamlin	73	74	73	75	295	3,173
Michelle McGann	78	70	75	69	292	7,237	Kathy Postlewait	72	73	75	75	295	3,173
Sharon Barrett	69	77	72	74	292	7,237	Barbara Mucha	73	73	73	76	295	3,173
Lori Garbacz	75	75	72	71	293	6,304	Jan Stephenson	73	72	74	76	295	3,173

The LPGA
Championship

The 1993 Mazda LPGA Championship

10 - 13 JUNE • BETHESDA COUNTRY CLUB, BETHESDA, MARYLAND

Trish Johnson was Number One on the LPGA Money List

It was more than eight months since Europe's dramatic Solheim Cup victory at Dalmahoy but the shock waves hadn't ceased to reverberate across the Atlantic on the LPGA Tour. Helen Alfredsson's Spring triumph in the Dinah Shore had been followed by back-to-back successes for England's Trish Johnson (her first ever wins in America) and in May Laura Davies won the McDonald's Championship (at the time, probably the nearest thing to a Major title, and even closer in hindsight given that McDonald's has now taken over sponsorship of the LPGA Championship).

As the players assembled for the year's second Grandslam event at the Bethesda C.C. in Maryland European golfers occupied three of the leading seven positions on the LPGA Money List, and, sitting atop the tree, was Trish Johnson.

Johnson was clearly one of the favourites to win the 39th LPGA Championship. The week prior to the event she was placed second in the Oldsmobile Classic, finishing just a stroke behind the winner, Jane Geddes. Maintaining that form, Johnson began her challenge at Bethesda with an excellent three under par 68, a score that was good enough for a share of the lead, albeit with nine others.

The second week of June, however, would prove to be something of a watershed on the 1993 LPGA Tour. European golfers continued to play well until the end of the season but it was as if the Americans determined at Bethesda that 'enough was enough'. Almost predictably, it was Patty Sheehan and Betsy King who led the US fight back – Sheehan eventually winning the LPGA Championship that week and King ultimately overtaking Sheehan to capture the end of season honours – but there was no shortage of surprises along the way.

The Peruvian-born golfer Jenny Lidback threatened to cause the biggest surprise of all when, after opening with a 69 at Bethesda, she added rounds of 67 and 68 to lead the tournament by two strokes on Saturday evening. Lidback had finished 124th on the 1992 Money List and hitherto hadn't shown any significant form so far in 1993. Sheehan was in joint second place after the

third day with Cathy Johnston-Forbes (they had compiled identical scores of 68-68-70). As for Trish Johnson, her hopes of victory had receded in the second round when she returned a 73. (In fact a closing 70 brought the English golfer into a respectable tie for eighth – the same position she had achieved in the Dinah Shore.)

Sunday, then, heralded a return to reality. A victory for Jenny Lidback might have happened in Fairyland but not, alas, in Maryland. Lidback scored a disastrous 78 on the final day and tumbled down the leaderboard to finish in joint 17th place.

Inevitably there were the last day charges, the most impressive of which came from Lauri Merten and

Jenny Lidback led the championship after 54 holes

Michelle McGann. A third round 66 had put Merten within sight of the leaders and when she followed this with a marvellous 67 on Sunday (her only blemish being to take three putts at the 13th) she set an eight under par target that only Sheehan looked capable of surpassing. McGann's climb up the

spectacular; there was a rather shaky finish too, but a round of 69, comprising 14 pars, three birdies and one dropped stroke was just sufficient for her to pass Merten and so claim her third LPGA title.

Merten wouldn't have to wait very long for her moment of glory but for now the

Back-to-back eagles for Michelle McGann (above) but a Major title for Patty Sheehan

leaderboard was spectacular for she scored successive eagles at the 12th and 13th holes but then quickly undid much of the good work by dropping shots at the 15th and 17th.

Sheehan's golf was measured rather than

hour belonged to Sheehan – as had much of the past 12 months: first the US Open; then the British Open (to secure a unique transatlantic double); then the Hall of Fame and now another Grandslam victory taking her into first place on the Money List. Dominant was the word.

1993 MAZDA LPGA CHAMPIONSHIP

10 - 13 JUNE • BETHESDA COUNTRY CLUB, BETHESDA, MARYLAND

Head and shoulders above her contemporaries – Patty Sheehan wins her third LPGA Championship

Name					Total	Money
Patty Sheehan	68	68	70	69	275	$150,000
Lauri Merten	73	70	66	67	276	93,093
Barb Bunkowsky	68	70	69	70	277	67,933
Betsy King	72	66	72	69	279	40,130
Michelle McGann	73	68	68	70	279	40,130
Tammie Green	71	69	69	70	279	40,130
Patti Rizzo	72	69	67	71	279	40,130
Nancy Scranton	74	68	72	66	280	23,651
Trish Johnson	68	73	69	70	280	23,651
Cathy Johnston-Forbes	68	68	70	74	280	23,651
Terry-Jo Myers	71	69	73	68	281	16,277
Kris Tschetter	73	72	67	69	281	16,277
Joan Pitcock	68	74	70	69	281	16,277
Jan Stephenson	69	69	73	70	281	16,277
Donna Andrews	70	72	68	71	281	16,277
Cindy Rarick	68	67	73	73	281	16,277
Jane Crafter	72	73	70	67	282	11,444
Nancy Ramsbottom	71	71	72	68	282	11,444
Jane Geddes	76	68	68	70	282	11,444
Elaine Crosby	71	71	70	70	282	11,444
Pamela Wright	68	72	72	70	282	11,444
Beth Daniel	74	67	70	71	282	11,444
Rosie Jones	71	71	69	72	282	11,444
Jenny Lidback	69	67	68	78	282	11,444
Kim Williams	72	70	72	69	283	8,947
Mary Beth Zimmerman	73	68	72	70	283	8,947
Nancy Lopez	68	73	72	70	283	8,947
Liselotte Neumann	72	68	73	70	283	8,947
Judy Dickinson	71	70	69	73	283	8,947
Angie Ridgeway	72	72	72	68	284	7,243
Chris Johnson	74	69	73	68	284	7,243
Dottie Mochrie	71	70	74	69	284	7,243
Alison Nicholas	70	72	70	72	284	7,243
Barb Thomas	72	69	71	72	284	7,243
Dale Eggeling	72	71	68	73	284	7,243
Cindy Figg-Currier	74	67	67	76	284	7,243
JoAnne Carner	69	73	73	70	285	5,609
Brandie Burton	74	70	70	71	285	5,609
Ayako Okamoto	73	71	70	71	285	5,609
Shelley Hamlin	73	66	75	71	285	5,609
Colleen Walker	73	70	70	72	285	5,609
Tracy Kerdyk	69	69	72	75	285	5,609
Jill Briles-Hinton	72	70	72	72	286	4,720
Lori Garbacz	72	71	69	74	286	4,720
Missie Berteotti	74	71	72	70	287	4,015
Suzanne Strudwick	73	71	73	70	287	4,015
Meg Mallon	71	70	73	73	287	4,015
Laura Davies	72	69	71	75	287	4,015
Kristi Albers	71	69	70	77	287	4,015
Danielle Ammaccapane	69	74	74	71	288	3,260
Kelly Robbins	72	69	76	71	288	3,260
Magie Will	70	68	71	79	288	3,260
Sally Little	74	70	72	73	289	2,731
Dana Lofland-Dormann	73	68	74	74	289	2,731
Tina Tombs	70	70	74	75	289	2,731
Stephanie Farwig	72	68	72	77	289	2,731
Karen Noble	74	70	73	73	290	2,203
Caroline Pierce	72	71	71	76	290	2,203
Pearl Sinn	70	72	71	77	290	2,203
Lisa Walters	73	70	78	70	291	1,901
Caroline Keggi	70	69	74	78	291	1,901
Hiromi Kobayashi	68	74	75	75	292	1,667
Stefania Croce	73	70	73	76	292	1,667
Nina Foust	69	76	70	77	292	1,667

US Women's
Open

1993 US Women's Open

22 - 25 JULY • CROOKED STICK GOLF CLUB, CARMEL, INDIANA

Crooked Stick: a splendid name for a golf course and a brave choice to host the US Women's Open. Designed by Pete Dye, Crooked Stick has a fearsome reputation; with its plethora of railroad ties some might even say that its appearance has more in common with the Wild West than the Midwest. This is where John Daly bludgeoned his way into the record books at the 1991 USPGA Championship. That same week one of the competitors suggested that a few of the par fives were so long it was 'necessary to take into account the curvature of the Earth'. How would the best women golfers in the world fare on such a course? Seventy-five thousand spectators turned up to find out.

Patty Sheehan was the defending champion following her thrilling play-off victory over Juli Inkster in the 1992

Helen Alfredsson made a bold attempt to win her second Major at Crooked Stick

championship at Oakmont. Sheehan was riding the proverbial crest of a wave having recently won the year's second Grandslam event, the LPGA Championship at Bethesda. A second player seeking a 1993 Major double was Helen Alfredsson, winner of the Dinah Shore in March. As things turned out, until she stood over a crucial 12 foot putt on the final green on Sunday.

'Alfie' enjoyed one of only three sub-70 rounds on the first day, her 68 earning her a share of the lead with Japan's Ayako Okamoto. Amazingly, her score included a seven at the par five 11th. Putting this

Sheehan put up a very reasonable defence of her title; for most of the week she was only on the fringe of contention yet still harboured a glimmer of hope as she walked to the 72nd tee. As for Alfredsson, her name stayed at or near the top of the leaderboard from the moment she birdied three of her first five holes on Thursday

setback behind her, she was able to finish as strongly as she began, recording birdies at four of the last seven holes.

If Okamoto's presence at the front of the field hinted that Crooked Stick might yield to a brilliant putter, we

(Left) Michelle McGann led the championship after a second round 66. (Above) Patty Sheehan

were again reminded of its reputation as a big-hitters' course when Michelle McGann returned a magnificent course-record 66 on Friday. Like Alfredsson the previous day, McGann – she of the dazzling jewellery and dazzling hats – scored seven birdies, and her 36 hole total of 136 gave her a two stroke lead over Alfredsson and a second Japanese player, Hiromi Kobayashi. Behind this pair there was another gap of two shots to

US Open. In short, she crumbled on Saturday. Three successive bogeys from the 1st meant her lead had gone; more problems followed and eventually she signed for a 78. It was shades of Patty Sheehan on the final day of the 1990 championship. But McGann, one suspects, will learn from the experience – as of course did Sheehan.

So which 'seasoned campaigners' were able to make a move on Saturday? Pat

Donna Andrews (left) tied for second place with Helen Alfredsson. (Opposite) Lauri Merten popped up from nowhere on the final day

former champions, JoAnne Carner and Jane Geddes, and Okamoto and Sherri Steinhauer. McGann led perennial title favourites Betsy King and Patty Sheehan by the considerable margin of eight shots.

It is often said that the third day of a Major championship is the most critical, the day for making a serious move. This is all well and good if you're a seasoned campaigner, sitting comfortably in the slipstream of the leaders, so to speak, but when you're inexperienced and the limelight is suddenly thrust upon you, it's a different matter. 23 year-old Michelle McGann wasn't used to leading tournaments, never mind the

Bradley scored a 68, the best round of the day, and three more former US Open winners, Laura Davies, Meg Mallon and Sheehan all scored 69s – but then so too did Helen Alfredsson.

The tall Swedish golfer was clearly playing just as well as she had at Mission Hills in the Dinah Shore tournament. In winning that event Alfredsson dispelled any doubts that her volatile temperament – there must be Viking blood in those veins! – would prevent her from coping with the unique pressure of leading a Major championship. Rounds of 68-70-69 had taken her to nine under par and with it a 54 hole US Open record (so much for Crooked Stick's fearsome reputation). On the eve of the final round she led the championship by two strokes from Kobayashi, and by three from Bradley and a player who had been quietly climbing the leaderboard, Donna Andrews. Nancy Lopez was four behind Alfredsson, and with Sheehan and Davies still in the frame, the 48th US Women's Open was heading for an exciting climax. As

overlooked? Simple: she hadn't won a tournament for nine years. Of course, with the benefit of hindsight, she was obviously building up to something special last July: she came third in May at the McDonald's Championship; second in June at the LPGA Championship...

On the 25th July – US Open Sunday – Lauri Merten produced the finest round of her life.

a violent thunderstorm gripped Crooked Stick on Saturday night, the one player that nobody seemed to mention as a possible winner was Lauri Merten.

Merten was only five shots out of the lead after 54 holes; why was her challenge

Poor Helen and poor Hiromi. The two leaders couldn't (as the saying goes) buy a putt in the final round. Kobayashi quickly fell away and Alfredsson was soon being chased by Bradley and Andrews. With birdies at the 8th, 9th and 10th Merten

started to surge through the field and even Sheehan made a late charge before eventually coming to grief at the final hole.

Although she couldn't 'buy any putts', Alfredsson wasn't making too many mistakes either. As she approached the final three holes it seemed that she might hold on after all. But Merten had other ideas. On the 16th, an extremely difficult hole, and one that Alfredsson would bogey, she chipped-in for a remarkable birdie. After safely parring the 17th she then struck a six iron to within three feet of the flag at the 18th. Merten's putter didn't let her down.

It all meant that Alfredsson now needed a birdie to force a play-off, and when her attempt from 12 feet on the last green slipped agonisingly past the hole it was all over. All over for 'Alfie', that is, but for Lauri Merten it had just begun.

Drama at the last: (above) Nancy Lopez birdies the final hole on Sunday; moments later Merten does likewise... and captures the biggest prize in women's golf

Lauri Merten wins the
48th US Women's Open

1993 US WOMEN'S OPEN

22 - 25 JULY • CROOKED STICK GOLF CLUB, CARMEL, INDIANA

Lauri Merten	71	71	70	68	280	$144,000	Michele Redman	75	71	72	72	290	8,334
Donna Andrews	71	70	69	71	281	62,431	Dawn Coe-Jones	69	72	76	73	290	8,334
Helen Alfredsson	68	70	69	74	281	62,431	Lori West	73	73	73	72	291	6,894
Pat Bradley	72	70	68	73	283	29,249	Alice Miller	73	68	78	72	291	6,894
Hiromi Kobayashi	71	67	71	74	283	29,249	Laurie Brower	73	73	72	73	291	6,894
Patty Sheehan	73	71	69	71	284	22,379	Julie Larsen	76	71	70	74	291	6,894
Betsy King	74	70	72	69	285	17,525	Amy Alcott	70	74	73	74	291	6,894
Michelle McGann	70	66	78	71	285	17,525	Cindy Mah-Lyford	73	73	70	75	291	6,894
Nancy Lopez	70	71	70	74	285	17,525	Shelley Hamlin	74	68	73	76	291	6,894
Ayako Okamoto	68	72	71	74	285	17,525	Kelly Robbins	71	70	74	76	291	6,894
Laura Davies	73	71	69	73	286	13,993	Dina Ammaccapane	71	70	70	80	291	6,894
JoAnne Carner	71	69	73	73	286	13,993	Debbi Miho Koyama	70	74	72	75	291	(Am)
Tina Barrett	73	73	70	71	287	11,999	Judy Dickinson	74	73	72	73	292	5,907
Chris Johnson	71	75	69	72	287	11,999	Michelle Estill	74	70	75	73	292	5,907
Sherri Steinhauer	73	67	75	72	287	11,999	Missie Berteotti	72	75	70	75	292	5,907
Nina Foust	71	71	71	74	287	11,999	Melissa McNamara	74	73	73	73	293	5,233
Dottie Mochrie	72	71	74	71	288	9,978	Cindy Rarick	76	70	74	73	293	5,233
Gail Graham	72	73	70	73	288	9,978	Elaine Crosby	75	70	75	73	293	5,233
Barb Mucha	75	69	71	73	288	9,978	Deb Richard	73	71	76	73	293	5,233
Kris Tschetter	73	71	69	75	288	9,978	Juli Inkster	71	72	76	74	293	5,233
Meg Mallon	73	72	69	75	289	9,061	Brandie Burton	74	72	72	75	293	5,233
Danielle Ammaccapane	73	74	73	70	290	8,334	Missie McGeorge	73	72	77	72	293	5,233
Allison Finney	74	72	73	71	290	8,334	Pamela Wright	73	73	74	74	294	4,412

The Weetabix
British Open

1993 Weetabix British Open

12 - 15 AUGUST • WOBURN G & CC (DUKE'S COURSE), BUCKS, ENGLAND

It is still hard to believe. How did she do it? It's not so much *that* she won but the way she won. That is what is so difficult to comprehend. Karen Lunn didn't just take part at Woburn, she took it apart...

Karen Lunn plots her path to an extraordinary triumph

and in the process annihilated a top class international field. It was supposed to be a European golf festival but Lunn turned it into an Australian golf procession.

The Weetabix Women's British Open is the flagship event on the WPG European Tour. Along with the US Women's Open, and perhaps also America's Dinah Shore tournament, it is the title that European golfers covet the most. That is why all the leading members of Mickey Walker's successful Solheim Cup team were present at Woburn last August. All present perhaps – though hardly prepared for the ensuing ambush.

There was also a formidable American challenge led by the defending champion, Patty Sheehan. Twelve months earlier Sheehan had become the first woman in history to win both the US and British Open championships in the same season. Moreover, she had since underlined her status as the world's number one player; firstly, by acquiring a sufficient number of US tour victories to secure admission to the LPGA Hall of Fame, and secondly, by capturing a third LPGA Championship at Bethesda in May. Joining her from across the Atlantic were Jane Geddes, winner of the 1989 British Open (as well as the 1986 US Open) and Brandie Burton, widely acknowledged as the rising star of American golf. A 'magnificent seven'?... Laura Davies, Helen Alfredsson, Patty Sheehan, Brandie

Burton, Trish Johnson, Lotte Neumann, Jane Geddes... These are the players whom Karen Lunn left trailing in her wake last August.

The personable Australian (whose confidence was apparently at such a low ebb at the beginning of 1992 that she seriously contemplated quitting the game!) didn't dominate from the outset – although she opened with a very promising two under par 71 – rather her form seemed to gather momentum as the week progressed. Two under par became six under; six under par

Putting woes for defending champion Patty Sheehan (far right) and Li Wen-Lin

became 11 under, and 11 under par... well, by Sunday she was an irresistible force... 11 under became 17 under. Her scores for those four rounds over the par 73 course were 71-69-68-67. Lunn was placed two behind the first round leader; then went one ahead of the field after 36 holes; she was five ahead after three rounds and finally won by eight strokes. She had company for a while then!

It came as no surprise when Laura Davies

led the championship after the first round. A huge gallery followed her, and an opening 69 gave the home favourite a one stroke lead over the Italian Federica Dassu and Li Wen-Lin from China.

Just as Davies' 69 was the only sub-70 score on Thursday, so too was Lunn's 69 on

Friday. The gallant Li Wen-Lin kept her second place by adding a 71 to her opening 70 to be just one behind, but even now the rest were beginning to string out. Davies disappointed her fans with a 76 and only

three others, Corrine Dibnah, Suzanne Strudwick and Kathryn Marshall found themselves within four strokes of Lunn after 36 holes.

Where were our 'magnificent seven' at this stage? Davies, Sheehan and Burton were all on 145 — still under par, in fact, but now five shots behind the Australian. Neumann was on 146; Johnson 147; Alfredsson 148 and Geddes was well down the field on 151.

It was the British Open and the weather at Woburn last August was typically British. Record crowds enjoyed four days of golf and the players experienced four seasons of weather. At one point there was a tremendous hailstorm but for much of the weekend there was beautiful sunshine and, with the Duke's Course in pristine

Laura Davies (right) led after the first round. (Below) Scotland's Kathryn Marshall

condition, the birdies flowed.

Three players achieved rounds of 68 on Saturday: Brandie Burton, Sweden's Carin Hjalmarsson and of course Karen Lunn. Aside from Lunn – who appeared to be playing a different course from everybody else – Burton's score was the most significant. It took her to six under par for the championship and into a tie for second place with Kathryn Marshall, a plucky Scot who produced a fine 69 in the third round.

With no disrespect to Marshall, Burton now looked to be the only player capable of catching the runaway Australian. Beyond Burton and Marshall was a gap of two strokes to Li Wen-Lin, while the defending champion Sheehan was a further two shots behind her.

Sunday was a glorious day – weatherwise and golfwise. As a contest it was all over after six holes. Lunn had already advanced her overnight score from 11 under par to 12 under when she rolled in a 30 foot putt for an eagle. For the hordes of sun-drenched

There were 68s on Saturday for Carin Hjalmarsson (top) and the eventual runner-up, Brandie Burton

*(Above left) Jane Geddes during her course-record 64;
(above and below) Karen Lunn at the final hole*

spectators, however, there was still plenty of golf to enjoy.

Europe's top players finally showed their form on Sunday. Laura Davies returned a 69, as did Trish Johnson, Catrin Nilsmark and Dale Reid. Helen Alfredsson scored a 71 and Marie-Laure de Lorenzi managed a 68. Only two players bettered the popular French player's score: one was 'you know who', the other was Jane Geddes, who smashed Patty Sheehan's one-year old course record with an incredible round of 64. The American fired 10 birdies and one eagle.

But no one could eclipse Karen Lunn's achievement. A run of four birdies in five holes on the back nine brought her home eight shots ahead of Brandie Burton. Geddes eventually finished in joint fourth place, but as for the rest of the 'magnificent seven', they trailed home between 14 and 24 shots behind the winner. And if they are the magnificent ones...

The day an Australian turned the golfing world on its head: Karen Lunn savours the moment

1993 WEETABIX WOMEN'S BRITISH OPEN

12 - 15 AUGUST • WOBURN G & CC (DUKE'S COURSE), BUCKS, ENGLAND

Player	R1	R2	R3	R4	Total	Prize	Player	R1	R2	R3	R4	Total	Prize
K Lunn	71	69	68	67	275	£50,000	S Gautrey	76	75	69	74	294	4,180
B Burton	75	70	68	70	283	32,000	C Duffy	75	76	71	73	295	3,880
K Marshall	73	71	69	73	286	21,000	R Hast	77	71	72	75	295	3,880
L Wen-Lin	70	71	74	72	287	14,350	J Soulsby	76	75	73	72	296	3,685
J Geddes	76	75	72	64	287	14,350	C Figg-Currier	75	75	72	74	296	3,685
P Sheehan	75	70	72	72	289	10,500	G Stewart	74	75	76	72	297	3,505
L Davies	69	76	75	70	290	7,300	P Meunier	73	76	77	71	297	(Am)
M L de Lorenzi	73	77	72	68	290	7,300	J Morley	77	74	74	72	297	(Am)
S Strudwick	72	71	73	74	290	7,300	V Michaud	79	73	70	75	297	3,505
C Nilsmark	76	71	74	69	290	7,300	T Abitbol	77	74	74	73	298	3,145
A Nicholas	74	73	70	74	291	5,400	F Dassu	70	75	75	78	298	3,145
T Johnson	72	75	77	69	293	4,670	X Wunsch-Ruiz	73	79	71	75	298	3,145
D Reid	76	75	74	68	293	4,670	D Hanna	74	73	73	78	298	3,145
C Hjalmarsson	77	74	68	74	293	4,670	K Cathrein	74	76	73	75	298	3,145
H Alfredsson	77	71	74	71	293	4,670	A Gottmo	77	70	74	77	298	3,145
S Gronberg Whitmore	76	70	79	69	294	4,180	N Buxton	74	74	74	76	298	(Am)
K Orūm	75	72	73	74	294	4,180	L Neumann	74	72	80	73	299	2,740

du Maurier Classic

1993 du Maurier Classic

26 - 29 AUGUST • LONDON HUNT & COUNTRY CLUB, LONDON, ONTARIO, CANADA

Rainy days and Sundays. This was a big tournament for Betsy King. As the final Major of the year it was an important event for all who had entered, but for King it was especially important. A first ever victory in the du Maurier Classic would not only put her on the threshold of the Hall of Fame (it would be King's 29th success on the LPGA Tour) but as a result she would also become only the second woman in *Betsy King bids for* history to achieve the *the Grandslam* modern Grandslam. King has won two US Opens, one LPGA Championship and is a two-time winner of the Dinah Shore tournament (and should the British Open ever establish itself as a genuine Major, then for good measure she has won that as well).

King began her quest for the du Maurier crown with a superb 65. But shooting brilliant opening rounds – and middle rounds for that matter – was not unusual for King in 1993; finishing the job on Sunday was the problem. It was now late August, yet for all her brilliance King still hadn't

Ping   Women's   Golf   Year

won in 1993, this despite leading on six occasions going into the final day's play. The Japanese golfer Hiromi Kobayashi (pictured below and winner of the previous week's tournament) was just one of several who had benefited from King's disappointing performances on Sunday.

There was a distinctly English feel to this championship. It wasn't the 'King factor' but because the 1993 du Maurier had brought the players to a town called London; to a classic parkland layout through which a certain River Thames ran and, yes, it rained just like at Wimbledon. But this was London, Ontario rather than London, England and to the delight of the home crowds it was a Canadian player who overtook King and produced the round of a lifetime on the opening day.

On her way to a course-record eight under par 64, Dawn Coe-Jones began her

Canada's Dawn Coe-Jones scored a sensational 64 in the first round; she followed it with a 74 on Friday, but recovered strongly on the final day. (Above left) Hiromi Kobayashi

round with scores of par-birdie-birdie-albatross (or double-eagle) to be five under par after just four holes! The albatross was the result of her holing a four-iron from 179 yards. It was a pity for Coe-Jones that she slipped to a 74 on Friday, for with rounds of 72-68 over the weekend she finished just a single stroke behind the eventual winner.

King, remember, had opened with a 65 and aside from Coe-Jones only two others bettered 68. By virtue of a 70 on the second day King took the lead and, with another solid round on Saturday, this time a 71 taking her to 10 under par, she found herself in the familiar position of leading the field with one round to play.

To use a typically English expression (though in the circumstances, a most appropriate one) King was 'far from home and dry'. Only a stroke adrift after 54 holes were Beth Daniel and Brandie Burton and a shot behind this formidable pair were three others including Dottie Mochrie. It was a high quality leaderboard and of all the season's Majors the du Maurier produced the most dramatic finish.

With eight holes to play King had increased her overnight lead to three and the Grandslam-securing win was now looking probable instead of possible. Daniel quickly dropped out of contention and with Mochrie also failing to mount a serious challenge, only the 21 year-old Burton seemed capable of catching King. When the young star birdied the 11th and King bogeyed the 12th the deficit was reduced to one. Things stayed that way for two holes then, incredibly, King four-putted the 15th green. Burton was now one ahead and following a stoppage for rain and a birdie at the 17th she went two ahead.

All over? Not quite... Burton contrived

to double-bogey the final hole and King actually faced a 15 footer for the title. But she missed it and at the first extra hole Burton rolled in a 20 foot putt for a winning birdie and her first Major victory.

Rainy days and Sundays. Somewhere in the sky there was a rainbow; Brandie may have glimpsed where it ended – but Betsy most definitely did not.

Victory! A glorious moment for Brandie Burton as her 20 foot birdie putt disappears into the cup at the 1st extra hole

21 year-old Brandie Burton captures the final Major of 1993

1993 DU MAURIER LTD CLASSIC

26 - 29 AUGUST • LONDON HUNT & COUNTRY CLUB, LONDON, ONTARIO, CANADA

Name						$	Name						$
Brandie Burton	71	70	66	70	277	$120,000	Rosie Jones	69	71	77	70	287	7,084
Betsy King	65	70	71	71	277	74,474	Dale Eggeling	70	73	73	71	287	7,084
(Burton won play-off at 1st extra hole)							Kristi Albers	70	72	72	73	287	7,084
Dawn Coe-Jones	64	74	72	68	278	54,346	Michelle McGann	67	74	72	74	287	7,084
Dottie Mochrie	68	69	71	71	279	42,269	Amy Alcott	70	70	73	74	287	7,084
Kris Monaghan	72	71	71	66	280	31,198	Kelly Robbins	76	71	72	69	288	5,317
Vicki Fergon	67	73	68	72	280	31,198	Lynn Connelly	76	71	71	70	288	5,317
Dana Lofland-Dormann	68	68	73	72	281	23,751	Jody Anschutz	73	74	71	70	288	5,317
Helen Alfredsson	70	70	72	70	282	19,926	Alicia Dibos	73	71	73	71	288	5,317
Kathy Guadagnino	69	69	70	74	282	19,926	Donna Andrews	73	71	72	72	288	5,317
Danielle Ammaccapane	72	72	73	66	283	14,894	Stephanie Farwig	71	73	72	72	288	5,317
Sherri Steinhauer	73	69	71	70	283	14,894	Missie McGeorge	72	73	70	73	288	5,317
Judy Dickinson	70	71	71	71	283	14,894	Hiromi Kobayashi	73	72	69	74	288	5,317
Chris Johnson	71	69	72	71	283	14,894	Lauri Merten	75	69	70	74	288	5,317
Gail Graham	71	72	72	69	284	11,674	Kim Williams	70	73	71	74	288	5,317
Tammie Green	69	73	72	70	284	11,674	Robin Hood	71	70	73	74	288	5,317
Lori West	72	72	69	71	284	11,674	Jane Crafter	74	71	73	71	289	4,106
Tina Barrett	74	72	70	69	285	9,862	Nina Foust	75	72	72	71	290	3,224
Deb Richard	72	74	70	69	285	9,862	Caroline Pierce	74	73	72	71	290	3,224
Sally Little	72	69	69	75	285	9,862	Lisa Walters	72	73	74	71	290	3,224
Beth Daniel	69	70	68	78	285	9,862	Martha Nause	71	73	75	71	290	3,224
Cindy Rarick	73	73	70	70	286	8,302	Colleen Walker	70	75	73	72	290	3,224
Nancy Harvey	75	70	71	70	286	8,302	Muffin Spencer-Devlin	71	72	75	72	290	3,224
Amy Benz	73	70	71	72	286	8,302	Allison Finney	73	71	73	73	290	3,224
Jenny Lidback	70	73	68	75	286	8,302	Karen Lunn	74	73	72	72	291	3,052

P i n g   W o m e n ' s   G o l f   Y e a r

The United States

1993 LPGA Tour Review

Betsy King may have experienced greater years, though surely none quite so extraordinary; Patty Sheehan might have experienced more extraordinary years, though surely none quite so great.

King and Sheehan were rarely out of the news in 1993. With both hovering near the magical 30 career victories mark at the beginning of the season, it was always likely that their exploits would capture the headlines. Thirty victories? Once a player has achieved the requisite number of Major title wins (and both King and Sheehan had) 30 LPGA Tour victories secures admission to the LPGA Hall of Fame — the most exclusive and prestigious club in women's golf. At the start of 1993 King had 28 wins to her name, Sheehan 29.

As for what happened to Sheehan in 1993 (as well as an insight into what continues to motivate her) the details are explored in a profile by Sonja Steptoe (page 78). Suffice to say that Sheehan won twice in 1993, the history-making title number 30 coming with her five stroke victory in the Standard Register Ping tournament at Moon Valley and, as if by way of proof that she has no intention of resting on those newly won laurels, title number 31 came less than three months later in the LPGA Championship at Bethesda.

Sheehan's career has certainly had its highs and lows and it is fair to say that her game has tended to blow hot and cold: brilliant one week, mediocre the next. Last year was no exception.

Betsy King's reputation is that of the supreme competitor. 'Steel' is her middle name. When King gets herself into a winning position she invariably goes on to win. At least, that's what we all believed at the beginning of the season. Betsy King became a mercurial golfer in 1993. She started to blow hot and cold — not in terms of her form varying dramatically from week-to-week, for she seemed to be challenging in almost every event she entered — but she would blow hot for two or three days at the start of a tournament only to cool down on the final day. Between mid March and mid September she was either leading, or joint leader going into the final day's play on no fewer than eight occasions — yet failed to win in every instance. It happened in the first Major of the year, the Dinah Shore and it happened in the final Major of the year, the du Maurier Classic.

Of course, if she had converted just two of those overnight leads into victories, she would have joined Sheehan in the Hall of Fame. Not only that, but she would have gone into the final event of the season with an unassailable lead in the Player of the Year standings and well clear in the race to become Leading Moneywinner. In fact, immediately before the LPGA Tour's last event of 1993, the Toray Japan Queens Cup

Sunday blues: it was an extraordinary year for Betsy King

Ping   Women's   Golf   Year

in November, King trailed Brandie Burton in the former and Sheehan in the latter.

So King was frustrated. And among those benefiting from that that frustration were Helen Alfredsson, Trish Johnson and Hiromi Kobayashi: three overseas golfers – and therein lies another tale.

Major prize winners: (Far right) Laura Davies captured the McDonald's championship; (above) Patty Sheehan claimed her third LPGA title and (right) Helen Alfredsson triumphed in the Dinah Shore

The LPGA Tour is not a 'World Tour' in the traditionally accepted sense, but in 1993 many tournaments had a United Nations-like flavour to them. Kobayashi won her first two events in America last year and there were also two Canadian victories, courtesy of Dawn Coe-Jones and Lisa Walters, but it was European golfers who made their presence felt the most.

The seeds were sown at Dalmahoy in October, 1992. Europe's shock win against the United States in the 2nd Solheim Cup match has had an enormous effect on the members of that successful team (and indeed on European golf generally). Naturally, all were inspired by the victory, but it has also greatly increased the level of self belief. A prediction was made in the first edition of this book: 'If confidence has a great influence on performance then it does seem likely that Europe's top players will go from strength to strength, climb the world rankings ladder and win more frequently.'

They certainly did that. Within seven days of Patty Sheehan's 'Hall of Fame' victory in March, Helen Alfredsson was winning her first LPGA tournament... the Nabisco Dinah Shore. Alfredsson thus became the second Swedish player to claim a Major championship (following Lotte Neumann's win in the 1988 US Open) and at Crooked Stick in July she very nearly became the second Swedish player to win the US Open. (Each of the 1993 Major championships is reviewed separately in Chapter Two).

Trish Johnson was next. A week after 'Alfie's' momentous achievement, it was the English golfer's turn to record her first American success by winning in Las Vegas. She won by an impressive four shots, and with a superb closing round of 67. Incredibly, Johnson won the following tournament as well, the Atlanta Women's Championship. American observers were astonished and it was around this time that Tom Tomashek commented in Golf World: 'The hottest piece of equipment designed to guarantee success on the LPGA Tour right now isn't an oversized driver, a graphite shaft or a ball with a zillion r.p.m spin rate. It's a European passport.'

It is not in Laura Davies' nature to watch quietly from the sidelines and her moment of glory duly arrived in May when she won the McDonald's Championship. It was her

fifth American victory. Then, a fortnight later another English Solheim Cup player, Alison Nicholas scored a spectacular 65 in the final round of the Corning Classic before eventually losing a play-off to Kelly Robbins.

The European dominance couldn't last forever and, apart from one or two

exceptions, most of the summer silverware was collected by golfers from America. As earlier mentioned, Sheehan won the LPGA Championship in June, and in July Lauri Merten (runner-up to Sheehan at Bethesda) was crowned US Women's Open champion, her first tournament win for nine years. Among those 'collecting silver' were Tammie Green and Meg Mallon who joined Sheehan, Johnson and Kobayashi as popular two-time winners.

One of the most intriguing and talked about aspects of the previous season had been the battle for hegemony between the so-called 'twenty-somethings' and the tour's more senior names: the emerging versus the established. The consensus felt it was 'honours even' at the end of 1992 and the same is probably true of 1993. There were no wins last year for Pat Bradley, Beth Daniel or Amy Alcott but both Sheehan and

King pushed their career earnings through the $4 million barrier, and Nancy Lopez took her tally of victories to 47, with a dramatic win in the Youngstown-Warren LPGA Classic. Lopez eagled the final hole to force a play-off, then defeated Deb Richard with a birdie at the first extra hole.

And what of the rising stars of the LPGA Tour? Donna Andrews and Michelle McGann made big impressions at the US Open (and elsewhere) and together with the consistent Sherri Steinhauer, Dana Lofland-Dormann and, of course, Lauri Merten, they are challenging strongly for places in this

year's Solheim Cup side.

Greatness would appear to be within the grasp of both Brandie Burton and Dottie Mochrie. At 21 years of age, Burton enjoyed nothing less than a sensational year in 1993. She won three tournaments, including her first Major championship (the du Maurier)

(Above) Pat Bradley explodes from sand.
(Above right) Dawn Coe-Jones gained her second Tour victory in 1993

Sherri Steinhauer couldn't repeat her 1992 win in the du Maurier Classic but enjoyed several top ten finishes

The next superstar? Brandie Burton's rise has been meteoric

and in the process became the youngest player to win a Major and the youngest and fastest to earn $1 million in prize money.

By the standards she set in 1992, Mochrie's year was slightly disappointing; at least, until she won the penultimate event of the season, the World Championship of

championships) in the next few years.

But we must end by rescuing Betsy King from her state of frustration. At the final hole of the final event of the season everything

(Below left)
Dottie Mochrie won in Naples but lost her Number One ranking.
(Below)
Michelle McGann

Women's Golf in Naples, Florida. Before then she had twice been defeated in play-offs she was expected to win: once by Missie Berteotti and once by the young English rookie, Helen Dobson. It will be interesting to see whether Mochrie or Burton wins the most tournaments (and Major

came right. A 20 foot birdie putt disappeared into the cup and King at last savoured victory. With that victory she overtook Burton to claim the Player of the Year Award and sailed past Sheehan to finish the season as Leading Moneywinner.

An extraordinary end to a great year.

1993 LPGA Tour Results

5 - 7 February
HEALTHSOUTH PALM BEACH CLASSIC
WYCLIFFE GOLF & COUNTRY CLUB, LAKE WORTH, FL

*Tammie Green	70	69	69	208	$60000
JoAnne Carner	66	72	70	208	37237
Brandie Burton	66	73	70	209	27173
Jane Geddes	72	71	67	210	16051
Chris Johnson	69	73	68	210	16051
Kelly Robbins	70	70	70	210	16051
Jenny Wyatt	66	71	73	210	16051
Kristi Albers	70	75	66	211	7993
Tracy Kerdyk	71	71	69	211	7993
Danielle Ammaccapane	71	71	69	211	7993
Dawn Coe-Jones	70	72	69	211	7993
Elaine Crosby	71	70	70	211	7993
Michelle McGann	72	68	71	211	7993
Tania Abitbol	71	69	71	211	7993

18 - 20 February
ITOKI HAWAIIAN LADIES OPEN
KO OLINA GOLF CLUB, EWA BEACH, HI

Lisa Walters	68	68	74	210	$67500
Nancy Lopez	68	67	76	211	41891
Dottie Mochrie	70	72	70	212	30569
Susie Redman	72	71	70	213	19624
Tracy Kerdyk	70	70	73	213	19624
Jane Crafter	73	66	74	213	19624
Dawn Coe-Jones	76	67	71	214	13360
Kelly Robbins	71	74	70	215	11208
Lori Garbacz	75	68	72	215	11208
Patty Sheehan	73	73	70	216	9057
Gail Graham	67	76	73	216	9057
Missie Berteotti	74	71	72	217	7245
Ayako Okamoto	73	71	73	217	7245
Marta Figueras-Dotti	73	71	73	217	7245
Laura Davies	70	70	77	217	7245

* Winner in play-off

11 - 14 March
PING/WELCH'S CHAMPIONSHIP
RANDOLPH PARK NORTH GC, TUCSON, AZ

Meg Mallon	67	66	70	69	272	$60000
Betsy King	70	67	65	71	273	37237
Jane Crafter	69	67	68	70	274	27173
Cindy Rarick	68	70	71	66	275	19121
Juli Inkster	70	67	71	67	275	19121
Pearl Sinn	69	73	71	65	278	11472
Alice Ritzman	71	72	68	67	278	11472
Nancy Lopez	70	66	72	70	278	11472
Hollis Stacy	73	66	67	72	278	11472
Kris Tschetter	69	74	69	67	279	6977
Lisa Walters	70	70	70	69	279	6977
Muffin Spencer-Devlin	69	66	73	71	279	6977
Patti Rizzo	69	70	66	74	279	6977

Lisa Walters retained her Hawaiian Ladies Open title

Trish Johnson scored back-to-back wins in April

25 - 28 March
NABISCO DINAH SHORE
MISSION HILLS COUNTRY CLUB, RANCHO MIRAGE, CA

(See page 29)

18 - 21 March
STANDARD REGISTER PING
MOON VALLEY COUNTRY CLUB, PHOENIX, AZ

Patty Sheehan	70	70	65	70	275	$105000
Kris Tschetter	69	71	71	69	280	56359
Dawn Coe-Jones	69	69	67	75	280	56359
Annika Sorenstam	73	66	72	70	281	36985
Tammie Green	73	69	67	74	283	29940
Dottie Mochrie	69	72	70	73	284	24656
Helen Alfredsson	71	72	72	70	285	19549
Robin Walton	69	73	69	74	285	19549
Brandie Burton	69	72	74	71	286	16555
Suzanne Strudwick	77	70	70	70	287	11237
Trish Johnson	70	73	74	70	287	11237
Lisa Walters	68	75	74	70	287	11237
Tina Barrett	72	72	72	71	287	11237
Jane Crafter	72	73	70	72	287	11237
Hollis Stacy	72	72	71	72	287	11237
Nancy L Ramsbottom	71	72	72	72	287	11237
Marta Figueras-Dotti	74	70	70	73	287	11237
Patti Rizzo	69	70	70	78	287	11237

2 - 4 April
LAS VEGAS LPGA AT CANYON GATE
CANYON GATE COUNTRY CLUB, LAS VEGAS, NV

Trish Johnson	71	71	67	209	$67500
Missie McGeorge	71	71	71	213	41891
Deb Richard	72	70	72	214	27172
Brandie Burton	74	65	75	214	27172
Hollis Stacy	73	72	70	215	16152
Lauri Merten	74	67	74	215	16152
Judy Dickinson	71	69	75	215	16152
Caroline Pierce	74	73	69	216	11775
Michelle Mackall	77	68	72	217	8264
Shelley Hamlin	75	70	72	217	8264
Carolyn Hill	74	71	72	217	8264
Amy Benz	73	72	72	217	8264
Annika Sorenstam	73	70	74	217	8264
Patty Sheehan	72	69	76	217	8264
Elaine Crosby	72	68	77	217	8264

P i n g   W o m e n ' s   G o l f   Y e a r

15 - 18 April
ATLANTA WOMEN'S CHAMPIONSHIP
EAGLE'S LANDING COUNTRY CLUB
STOCKBRIDGE, GA

Trish Johnson	72	72	68	70	282	$90000
Sherri Steinhauer	71	70	72	71	284	55855
Michelle McGann	74	68	72	71	285	40759
Missie Berteotti	74	69	78	65	286	26166
Elaine Crosby	71	72	74	69	286	26166
Betsy King	72	67	73	74	286	26166
Sherri Turner	76	67	71	73	287	17813
Dina Ammaccapane	77	72	71	68	288	14190
Hiromi Kobayashi	70	75	73	70	288	14190
Jan Stephenson	73	71	70	74	288	14190
Kelly Robbins	70	77	66	76	289	11473
Pat Bradley	77	72	71	70	290	9359
Florence Descampe	72	74	74	70	290	9359
Nancy Lopez	70	77	72	71	290	9359
Judy Dickinson	75	71	71	73	290	9359
Kris Tschetter	72	70	75	73	290	9359

29 April - 2 May
SPRINT CLASSIC
KILLEARN COUNTRY CLUB, TALLAHASSEE, FL

Kristi Albers	66	69	72	72	279	$180000
Rosie Jones	72	70	71	67	280	111711
Elaine Crosby	74	69	71	68	282	59629
Michelle McGann	72	72	69	69	282	59629
Deb Richard	70	74	67	71	282	59629
Kris Tschetter	71	70	70	71	282	59629
Jan Stephenson	71	69	73	70	283	31802
Liselotte Neumann	69	73	68	73	283	31802
JoAnne Carner	72	65	71	75	283	31802
Nancy Lopez	73	70	71	70	284	21023
Pat Bradley	71	72	71	70	284	21023
Sherri Turner	74	68	71	71	284	21023
Nancy L Ramsbottom	70	71	72	71	284	21023
Patty Sheehan	73	69	70	72	284	21023
Hiromi Kobayashi	69	70	73	72	284	21023

7 - 9 May
SARA LEE CLASSIC
HERMITAGE GOLF COURSE, OLD HICKORY, TN

*Meg Mallon	67	68	70	205	$78750
Tina Tombs	70	71	64	205	48873
Dana Lofland-Dormann	66	70	70	206	35664
Dawn Coe-Jones	64	76	67	207	21068
Hiromi Kobayashi	69	70	68	207	21068
Brandie Burton	70	68	69	207	21068
Betsy King	67	69	71	207	21068
Barb Bunkowsky	71	70	67	208	11821
Val Skinner	69	72	67	208	11821
Dottie Mochrie	71	67	70	208	11821
Ayako Okamoto	65	71	72	208	11821
Tracy Kerdyk	72	67	70	209	8453
Danielle Ammaccapane	72	67	70	209	8453
Amy Reid	68	71	70	209	8453
Lisa Walters	68	68	73	209	8453

*Former US Women's
Open champion
Meg Mallon gained two
early season victories*

13 - 16 May
McDONALD'S CHAMPIONSHIP
DU PONT COUNTRY CLUB, WILMINGTON, DE

Laura Davies	66	69	73	69	277	$135000
Sherri Steinhauer	69	72	70	67	278	83783
Helen Alfredsson	74	68	70	67	279	54346
Lauri Merten	68	69	72	70	279	54346
Hiromi Kobayashi	72	71	69	68	280	38494
Pat Bradley	73	70	71	67	281	25814
Mary Beth Zimmerman	72	74	65	70	281	25814
Patty Sheehan	68	73	70	70	281	25814
Gail Graham	66	69	74	72	281	25814
Chris Johnson	71	74	71	66	282	16756
Nancy Lopez	73	69	70	70	282	16756
Val Skinner	70	70	72	70	282	16756
Hollis Stacy	73	67	70	72	282	16756
Betsy King	71	67	78	67	283	12793
Alison Nicholas	73	74	67	69	283	12793
Dale Eggeling	70	76	68	69	283	12793
Akiko Fukushima	72	69	68	74	283	12793

21 - 23 May
LADY KEYSTONE OPEN
HERSHEY COUNTRY CLUB, HERSHEY, PA

Val Skinner	70	73	67	210	$60000
Betsy King	70	72	70	212	37237
Julie Larsen	69	72	72	213	27173
Tina Barrett	69	74	71	214	19121
Brandie Burton	68	71	75	214	19121
Cindy Figg-Currier	73	71	71	215	14089
Barbara Mucha	76	72	68	216	11170
Barb Thomas	71	74	71	216	11170
Dawn Coe-Jones	72	76	69	217	8155
Beth Daniel	71	75	71	217	8155
Angie Ridgeway	71	74	72	217	8155
Pearl Sinn	71	72	74	217	8155

27 - 30 May
LPGA CORNING CLASSIC
CORNING COUNTRY CLUB, CORNING, NY

*Kelly Robbins	70	68	70	69	277	$75000
Alison Nicholas	71	70	71	65	277	46546
Jane Crafter	73	70	72	67	282	33966
Patty Sheehan	72	70	72	69	283	26418
Tina Barrett	75	67	72	70	284	19499
Hiromi Kobayashi	71	68	73	72	284	19499

Cindy Rarick	73	73	71	68	285	13250
Tammie Green	72	70	73	70	285	13250
Jenny Lidback	74	69	71	71	285	13250
Trish Johnson	74	69	75	68	286	10087
Rosie Jones	75	68	71	72	286	10087

3 - 6 June
OLDSMOBILE CLASSIC
WALNUT HILLS COUNTRY CLUB, EAST LANSING, MI

Jane Geddes	72	68	68	69	277	$82500
Tammie Green	69	69	71	69	278	39208
Trish Johnson	71	66	71	70	278	39208
Alice Ritzman	66	70	71	71	278	39208
Nancy Scranton	71	71	69	68	279	21448
Betsy King	68	68	71	72	279	21448
Sherri Steinhauer	70	71	72	67	280	15359
Colleen Walker	67	72	71	70	280	15359
Beth Daniel	72	69	70	71	282	12316
Meg Mallon	69	70	72	71	282	12316
Cindy Rarick	72	69	72	70	283	10130
Elaine Crosby	69	72	72	70	283	10130

10 - 13 June
MAZDA LPGA CHAMPIONSHIP
BETHESDA COUNTRY CLUB, BETHESDA, MD

(See page 35)

17 - 20 June
ROCHESTER INTERNATIONAL
LOCUST HILL COUNTRY CLUB, PITTSFORD, NY

Tammie Green	74	69	63	70	276	$75000
Patty Sheehan	69	72	68	68	277	46546
Helen Alfredsson	68	75	67	68	278	30192
Kelly Robbins	70	71	66	71	278	30192
Dottie Mochrie	71	71	67	70	279	19499
Alice Ritzman	70	71	68	70	279	19499
Meg Mallon	71	67	72	70	280	13963
Barb Bunkowsky	69	71	69	71	280	13963
Lynn Connelly	70	66	74	71	281	10651
Beth Daniel	68	68	73	72	281	10651
Jenny Lidback	67	69	72	73	281	10651
Brandie Burton	68	72	70	72	282	8806

* Winner in play-off

25 - 27 June
SHOPRITE LPGA CLASSIC
GREATE BAY RESORT & COUNTRY CLUB
SOMERS POINT, NJ

Shelley Hamlin	67	67	70	204	$67500
Judy Dickinson	69	70	67	206	32078
Amy Benz	72	66	68	206	32078
Beth Daniel	70	67	69	206	32078
Martha Faulconer	71	68	68	207	17548
Danielle Ammaccapane	69	69	69	207	17548
Brandie Burton	67	74	67	208	12567
Anne-Marie Palli	67	73	68	208	12567
Angie Ridgeway	72	70	67	209	10076
Missie McGeorge	71	67	71	209	10076
Nancy Lopez	71	72	67	210	8023
Dale Eggeling	70	71	69	210	8023
Jane Geddes	69	70	71	210	8023

2 - 4 July
JAMIE FARR TOLEDO CLASSIC
HIGHLAND MEADOWS GOLF CLUB, SYLVANIA, OH

Brandie Burton	68	66	67	201	$67500
Hollis Stacy	67	67	68	202	41891
Jane Geddes	68	64	71	203	30569
Patty Sheehan	70	66	69	205	23776
Colleen Walker	68	71	68	207	16152
Amy Benz	67	71	69	207	16152
Suzanne Strudwick	67	70	70	207	16152
Marianne Morris	74	69	65	208	10132
Michelle McGann	70	70	68	208	10132
Dale Eggeling	70	70	68	208	10132
Judy Dickinson	69	69	70	208	10132

9 - 11 July
YOUNGSTOWN-WARREN LPGA CLASSIC
AVALON LAKES GOLF COURSE, WARREN, OH

*Nancy Lopez	68	68	67	203	$75000
Deb Richard	67	69	67	203	46546
Pat Bradley	73	66	65	204	24845
Deborah McHaffie	69	70	65	204	24845
Hollis Stacy	69	68	67	204	24845
Missie McGeorge	65	69	70	204	24845
Donna Andrews	70	71	65	206	12579
Kim Williams	70	67	69	206	12579
Rosie Jones	67	70	69	206	12579
Karen Lunn	66	68	72	206	12579

Shelley Hamlin

15 - 18 July
JAL BIG APPLE CLASSIC
WYKAGYL COUNTRY CLUB, NEW ROCHELLE, NY

Hiromi Kobayashi	69	71	69	69	278	$90000
Rosie Jones	72	71	68	71	282	55855
Betsy King	71	69	68	75	283	40759
Danielle Ammaccapane	72	70	73	70	285	28682
Jan Stephenson	72	72	68	73	285	28682
Helen Alfredsson	74	70	70	73	287	21134
Barb Bunkowsky	73	70	74	71	288	15901
Julie Larsen	73	68	75	72	288	15901
Kristi Albers	72	67	77	72	288	15901
Nancy Lopez	72	73	70	74	289	12082
Tammie Green	69	73	73	74	289	12082
Jane Geddes	68	77	75	70	290	10275
Juli Inkster	74	72	70	74	290	10275

* Winner in play-off

22 - 25 July
US WOMEN'S OPEN
CROOKED STICK GOLF CLUB, CARMEL, IN

(See page 43)

29 July - 1 August
PING/WELCH'S CHAMPIONSHIP
BLUE HILL COUNTRY CLUB, CANTON, MA

*Missie Berteotti	73	66	69	68	276	$67500
Dottie Mochrie	71	69	70	66	276	41891
Danielle Ammaccapane	70	72	68	68	278	30569
Helen Alfredsson	69	67	72	71	279	21511
Donna Andrews	71	68	66	74	279	21511
Laura Davies	72	68	71	69	280	14605
Trish Johnson	68	71	72	69	280	14605
Kris Monaghan	72	72	70	67	281	9691
Brandie Burton	71	71	70	69	281	9691
Amy Benz	71	71	70	69	281	9691
Pat Bradley	69	73	68	71	281	9691
Val Skinner	69	71	68	73	281	9691

Dana Lofland-Dormann

5 - 8 August
McCALL'S LPGA CLASSIC
AT STRATTON MOUNTAIN
STRATTON MOUNTAIN COUNTRY CLUB
STRATTON MOUNTAIN, VT

Dana Lofland-Dormann	63	73	70	69	275	$75000
Donna Andrews	71	69	67	69	276	46546
Deb Richard	71	73	68	67	279	33966
Michelle McGann	71	73	67	70	281	23902
Mary Beth Zimmerman	70	68	72	71	281	23902
Sherri Steinhauer	74	70	70	68	282	15179
Lisa Kiggens	73	70	69	70	282	15179
Patti Rizzo	71	70	71	70	282	15179
Kris Monaghan	74	71	68	70	283	10666
Nancy Lopez	71	70	70	72	283	10666
Brandie Burton	73	67	69	74	283	10666

Hiromi Kobayashi
and the biggest smile
in women's golf

12 - 15 August
SUN-TIMES CHALLENGE
WHITE EAGLE GOLF CLUB, NAPERVILLE, IL

Cindy Schreyer	67	68	66	71	272	$71250
Betsy King	67	67	67	72	273	44219
Gail Graham	67	73	67	68	275	32268
Dale Eggeling	68	71	67	70	276	20714
Kris Monaghan	66	69	70	71	276	20714
Marta Figueras-Dotti	69	65	71	71	276	20714
Allison Finney	67	71	71	69	278	13265
Dottie Mochrie	69	66	71	72	278	13265

20 - 22 August
MINNESOTA LPGA CLASSIC
EDINBURGH USA GOLF COURSE
BROOKLYN PARK, MN

*Hiromi Kobayashi	73	67	65	205	$67500
Cindy Rarick	67	69	69	205	41891
Tina Barrett	68	72	66	206	30569
Dana Lofland-Dormann	66	72	69	207	23776
Jill Briles-Hinton	70	70	68	208	17548
Jane Crafter	72	66	70	208	17548
Amy Alcott	70	72	68	210	12567
Jody Anschutz	71	66	73	210	12567

26 - 29 August
DU MAURIER LTD CLASSIC
LONDON HUNT & COUNTRY CLUB
LONDON, ONTARIO, CANADA

(See page 57)

4 - 6 September
STATE FARM RAIL CLASSIC
RAIL GOLF CLUB, SPRINGFIELD, IL

*Helen Dobson	67	65	71	203	$75000
Dottie Mochrie	67	68	68	203	46546
Jean Zedlitz	68	69	68	205	33966
Nancy Lopez	70	70	67	207	23902
Page Dunlap	69	69	69	207	23902
Lynn Connelly	73	68	67	208	11825
Hollis Stacy	72	68	68	208	11825
Rosie Jones	73	66	69	208	11825
Lauri Merten	70	69	69	208	11825
Tammie Green	68	71	69	208	11825
Danielle Ammaccapane	67	71	70	208	11825
Betsy King	71	66	71	208	11825
Amy Alcott	69	67	72	208	11825

10 - 12 September
PING-CELLULAR ONE LPGA CHAMPIONSHIP
COLUMBIA EDGEWATER COUNTRY CLUB
PORTLAND, OR

Donna Andrews	69	69	70	208	$67500
Missie McGeorge	69	69	71	209	36230
Tina Barrett	66	70	73	209	36230
Meg Mallon	69	69	72	210	23776
Betsy King	71	65	75	211	19247
Barb Mucha	70	73	69	212	14605
Danielle Ammaccapane	67	71	74	212	14605
Dottie Mochrie	74	72	67	213	8689
Jane Crafter	70	75	68	213	8689
Rosie Jones	73	70	70	213	8689

16 - 19 September
SAFECO CLASSIC
MERIDIAN VALLEY COUNTRY CLUB, KENT, WA

Brandie Burton	68	68	73	65	274	$67500
Rosie Jones	70	67	67	71	275	41891
Patty Sheehan	73	70	67	69	279	30569
Kris Monaghan	69	71	68	72	280	21511
Lauri Merten	72	66	70	72	280	21511
Dottie Mochrie	72	70	72	67	281	12906
Nancy Scranton	72	70	70	69	281	12906
Jenny Lidback	68	76	66	71	281	12906
Amy Benz	72	65	73	71	281	12906

After a series of second place finishes, Donna Andrews finally broke through and captured her first Tour victory

* Winner in play-off

Dottie Mochrie returned to winning ways in October

23 - 26 September
KYOCERA INAMORI CLASSIC
STARDUST COUNTRY CLUB, SAN DIEGO, CA

Kris Monaghan	66	69	69	71	275	$63750
Juli Inkster	69	68	69	70	276	39564
Patty Sheehan	69	66	70	73	278	28871
Dawn Coe-Jones	70	72	72	65	279	22455
Lauri Merten	70	72	71	68	281	16574
Pat Bradley	69	77	66	69	281	16574
Jane Geddes	72	71	70	69	282	10692
Meg Mallon	69	72	71	70	282	10692
Michelle McGann	74	70	67	71	282	10692
Donna Andrews	66	72	68	76	282	10692

14 - 17 October
WORLD CHAMPIONSHIP OF WOMEN'S GOLF
NAPLES NATIONAL GOLF CLUB, NAPLES, FL

Dottie Mochrie	72	71	68	72	283	$102500
Donna Andrews	72	74	70	69	285	31600
Michelle McGann	69	74	73	69	285	31600
Sherri Steinhauer	78	69	67	71	285	31600
Meg Mallon	67	74	73	71	285	31600
Nancy Lopez	70	75	69	72	286	14100
Lauri Merten	70	71	72	74	287	13800
Betsy King	73	71	73	73	290	13600
Brandie Burton	77	73	70	71	291	13400

Trish Johnson	70	76	75	71	292	13100
Helen Alfredsson	78	67	73	74	292	13100
Hiromi Kobayashi	70	75	71	77	293	12800
Tammie Green	76	74	71	74	295	12600
Rosie Jones	76	73	71	77	297	12300
Laura Davies	72	72	72	81	297	12300
Patty Sheehan	78	77	72	72	299	12000

5 - 7 November
TORAY JAPAN QUEENS CUP
LIONS COUNTRY CLUB
HYOGO-KEN, JAPAN

Betsy King	68	70	67	205	$97500
Jane Geddes	70	70	66	206	60510
Trish Johnson	70	68	69	207	35433
Dana Lofland-Dormann	69	68	70	207	35433
Dale Eggeling	70	66	71	207	35433
Brandie Burton	70	68	72	210	21096
Jan Stephenson	68	69	73	210	21096
Laura Davies	67	72	72	211	14645
Deb Richard	67	71	73	211	14645
Alison Nicholas	67	71	73	211	14645
Tina Barrett	69	67	75	211	14645
Toshimi Kimura	76	67	69	212	10827
Chris Johnson	70	72	70	212	10827
Suzuko Maeda	67	70	75	212	10827

1993 · LPGA WINNERS SUMMARY

HEALTHSOUTH PALM BEACH CLASSIC	Tammie Green	JAMIE FARR TOLEDO CLASSIC	Brandie Burton
ITOKI HAWAIIAN LADIES OPEN	Lisa Walters	YOUNGSTOWN-WARREN CLASSIC	Nancy Lopez
PING/WELCH'S CHAMPIONSHIP	Meg Mallon	JAL BIG APPLE CLASSIC	Hiromi Kobayashi
STANDARD REGISTER PING	Patty Sheehan	US WOMEN'S OPEN	Lauri Merten
NABISCO DINAH SHORE	Helen Alfredsson	PING/WELCH'S CLASSIC	Missie Berteotti
LAS VEGAS INTERNATIONAL	Trish Johnson	MCCALL'S LPGA CLASSIC	
ATLANTA WOMEN'S CHAMPIONSHIP	Trish Johnson	AT STRATTON MOUNTAIN	Dana Lofland-Dormann
SPRINT CLASSIC	Kristi Albers	SUN-TIMES CHALLENGE	Cindy Schreyer
SARA LEE CLASSIC	Meg Mallon	MINNESOTA CLASSIC	Hiromi Kobayashi
MCDONALD'S CHAMPIONSHIP	Laura Davies	DU MAURIER LTD CLASSIC	Brandie Burton
LADY KEYSTONE OPEN	Val Skinner	STATE FARM RAIL CHARITY CLASSIC	Helen Dobson
LPGA CORNING CLASSIC	Kelly Robbins	PING-CELLULAR ONE CHAMPIONSHIP	Donna Andrews
JCPENNEY/LPGA SKINS GAME	Betsy King	SAFECO CLASSIC	Brandie Burton
OLDSMOBILE CLASSIC	Jane Geddes	KYOCERA INAMORI CLASSIC	Kris Monaghan
MAZDA LPGA CHAMPIONSHIP	Patty Sheehan	WORLD CHAMPIONSHIP OF WOMEN'S GOLF	Dottie Mochrie
ROCHESTER INTERNATIONAL	Tammie Green	NICHIREI INTERNATIONAL	US LPGA bt Japan LPGA 23-9
SHOPRITE CLASSIC	Shelley Hamlin	TORAY JAPAN QUEENS CUP	Betsy King

1993 · LPGA TOUR STATISTICS

ROLEX PLAYER OF THE YEAR

RK	NAME	POINTS
1	Betsy King	40
2	Brandie Burton	37
3	Patty Sheehan	32
4	Tammie Green	25
5	Trish Johnson	25
6	Hiromi Kobayashi	24
	Meg Mallon	24
8	Donna Andrews	23
9	Dottie Mochrie	23
10	Helen Alfredsson	21

VARE TROPHY
SCORING AVERAGES

RK	NAME	AVG
1	*Nancy Lopez	70.83
2	Betsy King	70.85
3	Brandie Burton	71.02
4	Patty Sheehan	71.04
5	Dottie Mochrie	71.09
6	Helen Alfredsson	71.40
7	Tammie Green	71.46
8	Donna Andrews	71.54
9	Kelly Robbins	71.59
10	Judy Dickinson	71.59

GATORADE
ROOKIE OF THE YEAR

RK	NAME	POINTS
1	Suzanne Strudwick	226
2	Karen Lunn	207
3	Helen Dobson	203
4	Tania Abitbol	198
5	Dina Ammaccapane	189
6	Amy Fruhwirth	138
7	Stefania Croce	137
8	Jean Zedlitz	129
9	Alicia Dibos	127
10	K Marshall/M Thompson	72

*Lopez not eligible for award as an insufficient number of rounds played

TOP 10 FINISHES:
B Burton

DRIVING DISTANCE:
L Davies

DRIVING ACCURACY:
N Ramsbottom

GREENS IN REGULATION:
D Mochrie

PUTTING:
L Neumann

SAND SAVES:
N Ramsbottom

BIRDIES:
B Burton

EAGLES:
K Robbins

ROUNDS UNDER PAR
D Mochrie

1993 · LPGA TOUR MONEY LIST: TOP 60

Betsy King

23	Kris Monaghan	208,987
24	Kelly Robbins	200,744
25	Kris Tschetter	196,913
26	Hollis Stacy	191,257
27	Pat Bradley	188,135
28	D Ammaccapane	187,862
29	Jane Crafter	187,190
30	Judy Dickinson	186,317
31	Missie Berteotti	184,553
32	Missie McGeorge	180,311
33	Elaine Crosby	177,726
34	Cindy Rarick	174,407
35	Amy Benz	166,968
36	Jan Stephenson	161,123
37	Lisa Walters	149,260
38	Dale Eggeling	145,789
39	Barb Bunkowsky	142,907
40	Beth Daniel	140,001
41	JoAnne Carner	134,956
42	Nancy Scranton	129,766
43	Val Skinner	129,665
44	Shelley Hamlin	129,447
45	Gail Graham	126,048
46	Mary Zimmerman	118,626
47	Juli Inkster	116,583
48	Alice Ritzman	113,992
49	Patti Rizzo	111,371
50	Chris Johnson	111,027
51	Alison Nicholas	101,203
52	M Figueras-Dotti	101,102
53	Colleen Walker	96,384
54	Cindy Schreyer	95,343
55	Nancy Ramsbottom	93,354
56	Barb Mucha	91,806
57	Liselotte Neumann	90,776
58	Helen Dobson	84,959
59	Julie Larsen	83,532
60	Jenny Lidback	82,136

1	Betsy King	$595,992	12	Michelle McGann	315,921
2	Patty Sheehan	540,547	13	Sherri Steinhauer	311,967
3	Brandie Burton	517,741	14	Nancy Lopez	304,480
4	Dottie Mochrie	429,118	15	Meg Mallon	276,294
5	Helen Alfredsson	402,685	16	Dawn Coe-Jones	271,978
6	Lauri Merten	394,744	17	Kristi Albers	263,483
7	Tammie Green	356,579	18	Jane Geddes	263,149
8	Hiromi Kobayashi	347,060	19	Tina Barrett	261,249
9	Donna Andrews	334,285	20	Laura Davies	240,643
10	Trish Johnson	331,745	21	D. Lofland-Dormann	234,415
11	Rosie Jones	320,964	22	Deb Richard	223,282

Patty Sheehan

AMERICAN GOLFER OF THE YEAR

A Profile by Sonja Steptoe

The record should speak for itself. Patty Sheehan has been the LPGA Player of the Year, a Sports Illustrated Sportsman of the Year and a Vare Trophy winner, at one time or another during her 13-year career. Mickey Wright admires her swing. JoAnne Carner says she can play any course well. Yet, Sheehan's misfortunes say more about the kind of golfer and person she is than her achievements or her peers ever could.

It is the weirdest of ironies: Sheehan's bad luck has actually been good for her. If she hadn't taken so many hard knocks over the years, the world might never have known that she has tenacity as well as talent. She could have gone down in history as just another intelligent golfer with a pretty swing and a lot of trophies in her case. Instead, we now know that Sheehan is one of golf's true survivors – always fighting, as she puts it, 'to turn negatives into positives.' With the battle scars to prove it.

The long fight finally ended in 1993. She earned more than $540,000, won her third LPGA Championship and climbed to the top of the women's world rankings. But none of it meant as much as her victory at the Standard-Register Ping, where she shattered a tournament record and, more importantly, collected her 30th win – her passport to the Hall of Fame. It was, quite simply, the biggest positive of all. 'From now on, my

name will be associated with the greatest players of all time.' Sheehan said.

She's been a fighter from the start. That's the way it is when you're the youngest, the only girl in a house with three older brothers who allow no whining. By age four, she was on the slopes with them in her hometown of Middlebury, Vermont, struggling to keep pace. Steve, Jack and Butch were all crackerjack skiers; Patty wasn't. But she was plucky; a real sport, according to her father, Bobo, who coached the US Olympic men's alpine team in 1956 and the Middlebury College football, baseball, ski and golf teams for many years. Over and over again, she would skid, trip and slide down the bunny slopes. And over and over again, she would pick herself up, dust herself off and start all over again. Bobo marvelled at her indomitable spirit. 'If she'd fall, she'd plant that pole down and trudge back up the hill, her jaw sticking out,' he says.

It wasn't long before Bobo's tough little daughter was one of the country's best junior skiers. The family moved to Reno, Nevada before she hit her teens, and in her first season out West she entered 11 races and won 10. Bobo was ecstatic about her success. But he was careful not to push until she really needed it. One such occasion was the moment at the start of the race she lost that first year in Reno. Her ski got caught as she charged out of the gate. She spun

around helplessly and started to cry. Bobo, who was standing near the gate, yelled, 'Get going!' And Patty took off, skiing as hard as she could. She wound up fourth.

Gradually, golf supplanted skiing as Sheehan's sporting passion. Thank Leslie Sheehan for that. As a toddler, Patty rode on the back of her mother's pull cart. When she was four years old she got her first cut-down club. The only trouble was, she hated the game. All those hours in the searing heat with nothing to do but follow a silly little white ball. It wasn't exactly child's play. Later, when she became her mother's caddie and learned to appreciate the joys and the challenges of the sport, Sheehan changed her mind. 'Mom introduced me to the fun in the game,' she recalls.

Leslie also taught her self-confidence and self-reliance. 'Keep plugging away and believing in yourself, no matter how your luck is running,' mom must have told her, because that's how daughter plays.

'In golf, you're the only one to blame,' Sheehan says. 'I take the attitude that I'm out here doing the best I can. And I'm the best in the world whether I get the approval from the outside world or not. I'm the only one I have to answer to.'

Tough talk. But deep down, she knows that she and everyone else is subject to the whims of fortune. That's partly why, in 1983, the year she was named Player of the Year, she bought and remodelled a $120,000 home in California and donated it to a foundation for use as a shelter for abused and neglected teenaged girls. Sheehan named it Tigh (the Gaelic word for house, pronounced 'tee') and visited at least six times a year, spending her time in the living room, talking to the teens about their problems, dispensing advice when asked and

learning the latest dances. Sadly, the foundation ran into financial difficulties and was closed in 1990. But Sheehan's generosity and compassion cemented her reputation as a kind-hearted soul and earned her a share of the 1987 Sportsman of the Year Award from Sports Illustrated.

Sheehan might have been able to lend the foundation a hand, had she not been distracted by her own housing crisis. In what was the first in a heartbreaking series of Sheehan hard-luck stories, the 1989 San Francisco earthquake levelled her Bay-area home. A few weeks later, she learned that she didn't have earthquake insurance. The $200,000 required to put the pieces of her home back together came out of her own pocket. By the time she started the 1990 season, Sheehan was out of sorts and essentially broke. She never forgot what Bobo and Leslie had taught her, though. She got going and promptly won three tournaments before mid-season.

At the US Women's Open in July of that year, she stood at 12 under par after 36 holes and seemed to be on course for a famous victory. But the thunder clouds that blew in overnight and washed out Saturday's play brought with them still more trouble for Sheehan. She and the other golfers played 36 holes on Sunday to make up the lost time. After shooting a 35 on the front side that put her nine strokes ahead, Sheehan and her game slowly unravelled. While the rest of the golf world looked on in sad amazement, she surrendered the entire lead to a charging Betsy King, who made up 11 shots and walked away with a one stroke victory. Afterwards, the sight of Sheehan bravely attempting to answer an interviewer's, questions on network television and then bursting into tears was almost too painful to watch. One journalist observing the scene seemed to be reading Sheehan's mind when he wrote: 'Golf was no fun at all that day'.

Of course, plucky Patty rebounded, winning two more events in 1990 and earning $732,618 for the season. But the

that period,' she says.

Time to get her house in order. So, after the repairs were done, she sold her home in California and moved back to Reno, near her parents. Then, it was time to confront her US Open demons. Two shots behind best pal Juli Inkster, with a hole and a half

memory of that US Open loss would haunt her for two more years. She was sidelined for much of the second half of 1991 with an injured hand. The involuntary sabbatical — another symptom of her rotten luck, she decided — made her uncharacteristically grumpy. Though she wasn't playing, she showed up at the US Womens' Open that year and snapped at reporters during a tense pre-tournament press conference. 'It was an unsettling time for me,' Sheehan recalls. 'I had to overcome a lot of psychological hurdles – bad memories and bad thoughts. I never quite felt one hundred percent during

to play of the 1992 event at Oakmont Country Club in Pittsburgh, Pennsylvania, Sheehan finally got a lucky break from the golf gods – who surely owed her one. The heavens opened and violent thunderstorms halted play. Another rainy US Open, another chance to get it right. The two hour delay was just enough time for a pep talk. 'It's time I showed some guts', she told herself in the locker-room.

The break also caused poor Inkster to lose her concentration and momentum. When play resumed, Sheehan birdied the 71st and 72nd holes to force a play-off.

Buoyant and supremely confident, she won the 18 hole contest the following day without too much trouble. At last, the famous silver trophy was hers to cradle. The victory also put her on the threshold of the Hall of Fame.

Sheehan wasted no time in pursuing title Number 30. 'It was a lot like trying to win my first tournament', she later said of the quest. 'But this time I had a lot more experience behind me.' It was the experience of having bested bad luck.

At Moon Valley in the Standard Register Ping, Sheehan opened with a pair of unremarkable rounds of 70. But something ignited within her on Saturday and she birdied eight holes en route to a tournament record round of 65 that put her atop the leaderboard. On Sunday, at the 13th hole, she made believers of the sceptics who clung to those memories of tournaments and times past. Holding a three shot lead, she dumped her third shot at the 480-yards, par 5 into a greenside bunker.

Despite her sterling play the day before and a comfortable lead, a palpable sense of foreboding wafted through the gallery. It is no secret what they were wondering: was this the beginning of another collapse for bad luck's favourite target? They held their breaths as the ball bounced off her sandwedge. When it landed on the green and rolled into the cup, the cheers could be heard all the way to Reno. Sheehan went on to win by five shots.

And so, it came down to this: with a stunning shot on the 13th hole, in her 13th season, she became the 13th member of the LPGA Hall of Fame and earned a place in golf history.

If you didn't know better, you'd think that she's been one lucky lady.

Amateur Golf in America

How does that phrase go?... 'When the cat's away the mice will play.' For the past few seasons Vicki Goetze has dominated the women's amateur scene, twice winning the US Amateur Championship. Early last summer she took the professional plunge, thus enabling one or two former adversaries to seize a greater share of the spoils.

Jill McGill captured the top amateur prize last year when she defeated Sarah Ingram in the final of the US Women's Amateur (see overleaf) although it was Ingram who emerged as probably the leading player of 1993.

Ingram won the US Mid Amateur Championship and the Southern Amateur and featured prominently in almost every event she entered. Two other star performers were Emilee Klein and Stephanie Sparks and both, like Ingram, collected two important titles. Klein won the Broadmoor Invitational and the North and South, and Sparks won the Western Amateur and the Eastern Amateur. The evergreen Carole Semple Thompson, who in 1994 should make an eighth appearance in the Curtis Cup, won the Transnational Championship. As for the Women's Senior title, that went to Anne Sander – for the fourth time – and Kellee Booth won the Junior Championship.

The college golf scene also waved farewell to Vicki Goetze in 1993. Her last major event was the NCAA Championships

which were held in her home state of Georgia. In 1992 Goetze had claimed the individual prize ahead of Sweden's Annika Sorenstam. She came fifth in 1993's event, finishing five strokes adrift of Sorenstam – not Annika though, for she had already turned professional – but Charlotta Sorenstam. Clearly... when Annika's away, Charlotta will play.

Sarah Ingram, winner in 1993 of the Southern Amateur and US Mid Amateur championships

US Women's Amateur Championship

Whenever and wherever the US Women's Amateur Championship is staged, memories are invoked of great champions past. The first name that is brought to mind is usually that of Glenna Collett Vare who won the championship a record six times between 1927 and 1935. Yet when the 93rd US Women's Amateur came to Chula Vista in southern California last August, most unusually, it was the achievements of the greatest woman professional that were being recalled. It was at the San Diego Country Club, Chula Vista that the incomparable Mickey Wright won her record equalling fourth US Women's Open title in 1964.

Twenty-nine years on, the winner of the 92nd US Women's Amateur was not at Chula Vista to defend her crown. The highly talented Vicki Goetze had very recently turned professional and in her absence there was no obvious favourite to win the 1993 championship. If there was a favourite, however, it was probably Sarah Ingram, especially after her performance in the opening round when she defeated seven-time Curtis Cup player, Carol Semple Thompson 6 & 5. In that match Ingram produced an amazing run of six successive birdies. She duly made it to the final, although Delphine Bourson of France (2nd round) and Wendy Ward (in the semi-final) came close to defeating her – both losing at the last hole.

Ingram's opponent in the final was Jill McGill, a 21 year-old who learned her golf at Denver's Cherry Hills. McGill was raised in Colorado but as a student at USC she was on 'home ground' at Chula Vista. Her toughest match en route to the final was against Leta Lindley in the 3rd round but she won her semi-final against Brittany Schaff by a comfortable 5 & 4 margin.

McGill got off to a fast start in the 36 hole final and led 4 up at lunch. McGill, who is nearly six feet tall, had the advantage of extra length but it was Ingram's normally first-rate short game that let her down in the morning. After lunch she rallied however and with two holes to play had reduced her opponent's lead to just 1 up. A grandstand finish from Ingram? Almost: she lipped-out from 15 feet for a birdie at the 35th and nearly chipped-in at the last from 18 feet. But nearly is never enough – and McGill became a worthy champion.

August 9 - 14
1993 US WOMEN'S AMATEUR
SAN DIEGO CC, CHULA VISTA, CALIFORNIA

QUARTER-FINALS:

J McGill beat K Pittman 4 & 2
S Ingram beat E Knuth 3 & 1
B Schaff beat P Pedersen 3 & 2
W Ward beat D Koyama 1 hole

SEMI-FINALS:

J McGill beat B Schaff 5 & 4
S Ingram beat W Ward 1 hole

FINAL

J McGILL beat S INGRAM 1 hole

· ROLL OF HONOUR ·

1895	Mrs C S Brown	1935	Glenna Collett Vare	1978	Cathy Sherk
1896	Beatrix Hoyt	1936	Pam Barton (GB)	1979	Carolyn Hill
1897	Beatrix Hoyt	1937	Mrs Julius Page	1980	Juli Inkster
1898	Beatrix Hoyt	1938	Patty Berg	1981	Juli Inkster
1899	Ruth Underhill	1939	Betty Jameson	1982	Juli Inkster
1900	Frances Griscom	1940	Betty Jameson	1983	Joanne Pacillo
1901	Genevieve Hecker	1941	Elizabeth Hicks Newell	1984	Deb Richard
1902	Genevieve Hecker	1942-5	No competition	1985	Michiko Hattori (Jap)
1903	Bessie Anthony	1946	Babe Zaharias	1986	Kay Cockerill
1904	Georgianna Bishop	1947	Louise Suggs	1987	Kay Cockerill
1905	Pauline Mackay	1948	Grace Lenczyk	1988	Pearl Sinn
1906	Harriot Curtis	1949	Dorothy Germain Porter	1989	Vicki Goetze
1907	Margaret Curtis	1950	Beverly Hanson	1990	Patty Hurst
1908	Kate Harley	1951	Dorothy Kirby	1991	Amy Fruhwirth
1909	Dorothy Campbell (GB)	1952	Jacqueline Pung	1992	Vicki Goetze
1910	Dorothy Campbell (GB)	1953	Mary Lena Faulk	1993	Jill McGill
1911	Margaret Curtis	1954	Barbara Romack		
1912	Margaret Curtis	1955	Patricia Lesser		
1913	Gladys Ravenscroft (GB)	1956	Marlene Stewart (Can)		
1914	Kate Harley Jackson	1957	JoAnne Gunderson		
1915	Mrs C H Vanderbeck	1958	Anne Quast		
1916	Alexa Stirling	1959	Barbara McIntire		
1917	No competition	1960	JoAnne Gunderson		
1918	No competition	1961	Anne Quast Decker		
1919	Alexa Stirling	1962	JoAnne Gunderson		
1920	Alexa Stirling	1963	Anne Quast Welts		
1921	Marion Hollins	1964	Barbara McIntire		
1922	Glenna Collett	1965	Jean Ashley		
1923	Edith Cummings	1966	JoAnne Gunderson Carner		
1924	Dorothy Campbell Hurd (GB)	1967	Mary Lou Dill		
1925	Glenna Collett	1968	JoAnne Gunderson Carner		
1926	Helen Stetson	1969	Catherine Lacoste (Fr)		
1927	Miriam Burns Horn	1970	Martha Wilkinson		
1928	Glenna Collett	1971	Laura Baugh		
1929	Glenna Collett	1972	Mary Anee Budke		
1930	Glenna Collett	1973	Carol Semple		
1931	Helen Hicks	1974	Cynthia Hill		
1932	Virginia Van Wie	1975	Beth Daniel		
1933	Virginia Van Wie	1976	Donna Horton		
1934	Virginia Van Wie	1977	Beth Daniel		

Jill McGill

Europe

4

1993 WPG European Tour Review

Storm in a Scottish tea cup? Hardly. Nor was it a three-day wonder. In the first half of 1993 Hurricane Dalmahoy was alive and well and wreaking havoc across the length and breadth of the United States. Europe's women golfers were not only amazing the Americans, they were amazing themselves with their stunning achievements on the LPGA Tour. So when these 'transatlantic heroes' returned to play in Europe – and they competed with varying degrees of regularity throughout the summer – charting their progress was never likely to be dull. However, if they arrived believing that there were easy pickings to be found, they were seriously mistaken. They certainly didn't dominate when they appeared, moreover, and it may seem an odd thing to state, but judging their performances collectively, the leading Europeans probably played better in North America than they did in Europe.

Golfers from 'Down Under' were partly responsible. Just as a small band of Europeans plundered some of the LPGA Tour's most sought after trophies, so a handful of Australians waltzed off with a choice selection of European silver.

More than one third of the events on the 1993 WPG European Tour were won by golfers from Australia, including of course the most important prize of all, the Weetabix British Open.

The other principal cause of the big names' failure to stamp their authority on their home circuit was the emergence (and brilliance) of four young players, two of whom were rookies and all aged under 25: Annika Sorenstam from Sweden, Spain's Amaya Arruti (they were the rookies) and Helen Dobson and Lora Fairclough from England. Of this quartet only Sorenstam failed to win a tournament – another irony since she was arguably Europe's Golfer of the Year, and is profiled as such by Patricia Davies later in this chapter.

It is no secret that the Tour experienced administrative turmoil at the beginning of 1993. Former Executive Director Andrea Doyle departed in less than harmonious circumstances (around the same time as Helen Alfredsson was winning the Dinah Shore tournament in America) to be replaced at the helm by Terry Coates. The limited schedule was the major concern among officials and players alike, and while it is beyond the scope of this review to analyse developments beyond the fairways, it is encouraging to see that a far greater number of events appear on the 1994 Tour calendar. There is still much to be done, of course, but the new Chief Executive appears to have made a very good impression and at the end of last season there was a bullish and buoyant atmosphere behind the scenes at Tytherington; hopefully the Tour will now flourish and go from strength to strength.

Not withstanding the administrative

upheavals and paucity of tournaments, those European events that did take place in 1993 produced some sparkling golf and, as noted above, unveiled many fresh faces on the winners rostrum. Equally welcoming was the fact that at the British Open and at tournaments in Sweden and Germany, record crowds watched the respective dramas unfold.

Before the 1993 season commenced in Europe a WPG European Tour event was held in January in South East Asia. The KRP World Ladies Classic was staged amongst the bougainvillaea at the Kelab Rahman Putra Golf Club in Kuala Lumpur. A strong field gathered and, given her modest form of the previous year, a surprise winner emerged when Karen Lunn defeated 1992's Rookie of the Year, Sandrine Mendiburu in a play-off. It is strange to reflect that the

She didn't win in 1993 and she occasionally strayed from the fairway, but Swedish rookie Annika Sorenstam was a revelation

P i n g   W o m e n ' s   G o l f   Y e a r

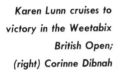

Karen Lunn cruises to
victory in the Weetabix
British Open;
(right) Corinne Dibnah

French player was probably favourite to win that play-off, for as Mendiburu went on to suffer a loss of form in Europe, so the Australian has never looked back after her victory in steamy hot Malaysia.

Some three and a half months after Lunn's Asian triumph, the Tour recommenced in the more familiar surroundings of Woburn. Nothing yet had happened in Europe, but European golfers were grabbing all the headlines in America. Both Laura Davies and Trish Johnson returned to England for the Ford Classic but for once it was Johnson whom everybody was fussing over. There was good reason for she had just won back-to-back tournaments in Atlanta and Las Vegas and was leading the LPGA Money List. The other outstanding early season performance in America by a European player was Helen Alfredsson's Major championship triumph at Mission

Hills. Alfredsson didn't appear in the Ford Classic but the spectators received ample consolation when they witnessed the extraordinary tour debut of her compatriot Annika Sorenstam.

After three rounds on the Duchess Course, the Swedish rookie led the field by two shots. Both Davies and Johnson trailed by five and they eventually finished tied for 5th and 8th places respectively. Early in the final round Sorenstam extended her lead to four and a famous victory looked imminent. Nerves, however, got the better of her (although she would probably never admit as much!) and over the closing holes she dropped several shots and was overtaken by Federica Dassu. Following Stefania Croce's win in 1992, Dassu thus became the second Italian to win the tournament.

The Holiday Inn Leiden Open in Holland was the Tour's next stop – and a very windswept stop it was. 'I was almost blown off my feet', said Corrine Dibnah, after she had gained a one shot victory. Laura Davies was again present — still slightly 'up in the clouds' after a superb win in the LPGA Tour's McDonald's Championship — and Annika Sorenstam was again runner-up.

Germany — and it heralded an overdue reunion for Europe's triumphant Solheim Cup team. All ten of Mickey Walker's side showed up for the BMW European Masters at Bercuit near

'Transatlantic hero' Trish Johnson came to Woburn in late April leading the LPGA Money List

Sorenstam finished just a stroke behind Dibnah. Davies' major achievement of the week was when she managed (admittedly with the wind gusting at her back) to drive the green at the 353-yards par four 11th! Third behind Dibnah and Sorenstam was Mardi Lunn, Karen's sister, and she wouldn't have to wait too long before she became the Tour's third Australian winner.

Commencing at the end of June, a 'mini tour' of three lucrative events took place on the continent — one in Belgium and two in

Brussels, and they remained for the Hennessy Ladies' Cup in Cologne. The party started to break up before the European Ladies' Classic in Bad Griesbach, although a quality line-up assembled nonetheless.

England's Helen Dobson emerged as an unlikely star of this mini tour. The adjective 'unlikely' was chosen, not because anyone has every questioned her enormous ability — Dobson enjoyed a brilliant amateur career — but because in her previous two seasons on Tour she had hitherto failed to live up to

Success in Belgium:
Helen Dobson savours
a magnificent triumph
in the BMW
European Masters

the enormous expectations. The 22 year-old began to fulfil those expectations in the final round at Bercuit when she came from five strokes behind overnight leader Marie-Laure de Lorenzi to capture her first professional victory.

One week later Dobson very nearly pulled off a remarkable double by winning the prestigious Hennessy Ladies' Cup. Teeing-off in the final round she again found herself five shots out of the lead, and again it was de Lorenzi whom she trailed (this time as joint leader with Laura Davies). Not a great deal happened during her first seven holes on Sunday but then she achieved a hole-in-one at the 8th (winning a £12,500 car in the process) and followed that with four birdies in the next six holes. A par at the last would have given Dobson a round of 65 and taken her into a play-off; unfortunately she missed a four foot putt at the final hole and so missed out by one.

It was two former US Open champions, Davies and Lotte Neumann who contested the play-off, and Neumann who triumphed with a birdie at the first extra hole. Her victory meant that the cup stayed in Swedish hands as Helen Alfredsson had been attempting a hatrick of wins in Cologne. Alfredsson in fact finished in a tie for eighth place, her hopes disappearing when she

Karen Lunn's magnificent victory. The Weetabix British Open is reviewed separately in Chapter Two, however, our picture of a final day leaderboard on page 90 provides an accurate summation. The detail reveals the full story of total domination.

There was more than a hint of

1993 brought glory in America for Helen Alfredsson, and a victory in Europe for Lotte Neumann (far left)

scored a 77 in the third round. So much for 'Alfie' but what of Annika? Sorenstam came joint sixth in Cologne, finishing a stroke ahead of Alfredsson and so providing further proof – if any more were now needed – that she could play well on a big occasion and in Solheim Cup company.

If there were questions concerning Sorenstam they were mainly as to *when* she would gain her first win. She came very close again in the European Ladies' Classic at Bad Griesbach, for she led going into the final round but was pipped at the post by Mardi Lunn. However, she did finish in front of Davies, Alison Nicholas and Catrin Nilsmark, and ahead of Helen Dobson whose great run was brought to a premature conclusion when an injury forced her withdrawal on the eve of the tournament.

After Mardi Lunn's fine victory came

dominance in the IBM Ladies' Open which immediately followed the spectacle at Woburn. Britain's Lora Fairclough – still still seeking her first Tour success – took on the mighty Swedes over their home ground in Haninge and strolled to a five shot victory. Corrine Dibnah was a distant second, and although eight of the 1992 Solheim Cup team were present in Sweden, and five Swedes were placed among the top ten, not one finished within six strokes of the winner. Apparently Fairclough was 'shaking like a jelly' as she played the closing holes. Unfortunately for the rest of the field she stubbornly refused to wobble.

Into September and only three tournaments remained to be played... and Laura Davies still hadn't won in Europe. Each year since 1985 she had managed to win at least once. The English Open at

Tytherington (headquarters of the WPG European Tour) seemed the perfect place for her to put matters right. The course suits her power game and she was also the defending champion, having stormed to victory by seven shots in 1992. After 36 holes, however, things weren't going to plan

Germany and now in England – she had been in a strong position with one round to play but had failed on the final day. If England's best player could win the English Open, maybe France's best player could win the French Open? The French championship was the final event of the 1993 season but

Mixed fortunes for France's Marie-Laure de Lorenzi (above) and Sandrine Mendiburu (right)

as Davies was six behind mid-way leader Marie-Laure de Lorenzi. But she hadn't given up hope and with a brilliant third round 64 Davies surged through the field and even overtook de Lorenzi, who had produced a far from shabby 71. The final day developed into a marvellous head-to-head battle and, in keeping with the script, Davies eventually sneaked home one ahead of her great French rival. The remainder of the Tytherington cast were nowhere to be seen.

Now it was poor Marie-Laure who had yet to win! Three times – in Belgium,

before it took place the destiny of the European Order of Merit crown and the Italian Open title had to be decided.

Karen Lunn still held a considerable lead at the top of the merit table, thanks in the main to the £50,000 cheque she received for winning the Weetabix British Open. Davies could still catch her, but she needed another victory. With this new goal in mind Davies entered the Italian Open at Lignano and for three days she played very well compiling rounds of 70-70-66. She should have been in with a great chance of winning on the final day but incredibly was six strokes behind Spanish rookie Amaya Arruti. The 22 year-old had scored rounds of 67-65-68.

*Laura Davies retained
her English Open title
in September but lost
her Order of Merit
crown to Australia's
Karen Lunn*

'Amazing Amaya' duly went on to secure a famous victory; this in only her sixth professional event.

One wondrous week couldn't deny Sorenstam her Rookie of the Year prize but it certainly put paid to Davies' chances of overtaking Karen Lunn.

So to the beautiful Var region of France and Marie-Laure de Lorenzi's bid to win the French Open crown. With 18 holes to play the home favourite lay three shots adrift of Gillian Stewart and Federica Dassu. Her hopes of a perfect ending to the year looked somewhat remote until fortune finally smiled on Marie-Laure, and with a courageous last day 69 she snatched the title.

On the other side of the Atlantic, Betsy King ended her own winless streak and brought the curtain down on the 1993 LPGA Tour in similarly dramatic circumstances. And so they took their bows, a King in America and a queen in France.

1993 WPG European Tour Results

14 - 17 January
KRP WORLD LADIES CLASSIC
KELAB RAHMAN PUTRA GOLF CLUB
KUALA LUMPUR, MALAYSIA

* Karen Lunn	69	70	74	73	286	US$45000
Sandrine Mendiburu	72	72	73	69	286	30450
Alison Nicholas	76	70	72	72	290	18600
Kim Lasken	71	78	70	71	290	18600
Suzanne Strudwick	77	69	73	73	292	12720
Laura Davies	76	70	73	74	293	9000
Lora Fairclough	73	74	76	70	293	9000
Lisa Hackney	71	74	69	79	293	9000
Corinne Dibnah	71	74	78	73	296	5480
Dale Reid	74	73	77	72	296	5480
Janet Soulsby	74	76	73	73	296	5480
Catrin Nilsmark	73	76	72	75	296	5480
Carin Hjalmarsson	72	74	76	74	296	5480
Kristal Parker	74	74	74	74	296	5480

29 April - 2 May
FORD GOLF CLASSIC
WOBURN G & CC (DUCHESS COURSE)
BUCKS, ENGLAND

Federica Dassu	72	73	73	71	289	£10500
Annika Sorenstam	71	72	71	76	290	7105
Laurette Maritz-Atkins	75	72	72	72	291	4900
Helen Wadsworth	72	70	74	76	292	3780
Laura Davies	76	74	69	74	293	2506
Regine Lautens	73	71	72	77	293	2506
Karen Lunn	75	71	73	74	293	2506
Trish Johnson	71	72	75	77	295	1572
Alison Nicholas	76	74	71	74	295	1572
Gillian Stewart	76	75	76	68	295	1572
Catherine Panton-Lewis	77	73	71	75	296	1288
Marie-Laure de Lorenzi	76	74	73	74	297	1116
Dale Reid	71	72	73	81	297	1116
Tina Yarwood	72	75	78	72	297	1116
Kristal Parker	75	75	73	74	297	1116

29 - 31 May
HOLIDAY INN LEIDEN OPEN
RIJSWIJK GOLF & BUSINESS CENTRE
NR ROTTERDAM, NETHERLANDS

Corinne Dibnah	67	73	74	214	£8250
Annika Sorenstam	72	70	73	215	5580
Mardi Lunn	69	71	76	216	3850
Laurette Maritz-Atlkins	69	75	73	217	2408
Susan Moon	70	68	79	217	2408
Lora Fairclough	71	71	75	217	2408
Lisa Hackney	69	74	75	218	1650
Laura Davies	72	71	76	219	1375
Veronique Palli	70	74	76	220	1230
Marie-Laure de Lorenzi	73	75	73	221	1019
Dale Reid	71	78	72	221	1019
Kristal Parker	76	70	75	221	1019

24 - 27 June
BMW EUROPEAN MASTERS
GOLF DU BERCUIT, BRUSSELS, BELGIUM

Helen Dobson	71	71	72	69	283	£22500
Marie-Laure de Lorenzi	70	69	70	75	284	12862
Dale Reid	71	73	70	70	284	12862
Pamela Wright	67	74	73	71	285	8100
Laura Davies	69	68	73	76	286	5370
Liselotte Neumann	71	68	75	72	286	5370
Alison Nicholas	70	70	72	74	286	5370
Janet Soulsby	73	71	71	73	288	3555
Li Wen-Lin	73	73	72	70	288	3555
Kristal Parker	72	72	72	73	289	3000
Annika Sorenstam	75	71	70	75	291	2670
Lisa Hackney	70	78	72	71	291	2670
Gillian Stewart	72	71	74	75	292	2370
Laree Sugg	72	75	74	71	292	2370
Trish Johnson	70	76	73	74	293	2220
Sally Prosser	74	70	74	75	293	2220

* Winner in play-off

An Italian double: Federica Dassu succeeds Stefania Croce as the winner of the Ford Classic at Woburn

Lotte Neumann has just defeated Laura Davies in a play-off for the Hennessy Ladies' Cup

1 - 4 July
HENNESSY LADIES' CUP
GOLF UND LANDCLUB KOLN, KOLN, GERMANY

*Liselotte Neumann	72	71	69	68	280	£30000
Laura Davies	70	68	72	70	280	20280
Helen Dobson	71	70	74	66	281	14000
Pamela Wright	71	70	70	71	282	10800
Karen Lunn	70	73	70	70	283	8480
Laurette Maritz-Atkins	73	69	71	71	284	6500
Annika Sorenstam	71	73	70	70	284	6500
Trish Johnson	71	68	74	72	285	4493
Florence Descampe	70	71	72	72	285	4493
Helen Alfredsson	68	71	77	69	285	4493
Alison Nicholas	74	72	70	71	287	3360
Catherine Panton-Lewis	72	71	69	75	287	3360
Julie Forbes	71	74	73	69	287	3360
Lisa Hackney	69	73	73	72	287	3360

* Winner in play-off

8 - 11 July
EUROPEAN LADIES' GOLF CLASSIC
GOLF CLUB, SAGMUHLE, BAD GRIESBACH, GERMANY

Mardi Lunn	74	70	69	74	287	£15000
Annika Sorenstam	70	70	72	76	288	10150
Mette Hageman	75	68	71	75	289	7000
Laura Davies	78	70	68	74	290	4380
Alison Nicholas	74	70	72	74	290	4380
Catrin Nilsmark	70	69	74	77	290	4380
Laurette Maritz-Atkins	76	70	69	76	291	2750
Carin Hjalmarsson	73	70	70	78	291	2750
Janet Soulsby	71	74	71	76	292	2240
Susan Moon	77	66	73	77	293	1920
Helen Wadsworth	72	75	73	73	293	1920

12 - 15 August
WEETABIX WOMEN'S BRITISH OPEN
WOBURN G & CC (DUKE'S COURSE)
BUCKS, ENGLAND

(See page 51)

Ping Women's Golf Year

19 - 22 August
IBM LADIES' OPEN
HANINGE GOLF CLUB, NR STOCKHOLM, SWEDEN

Lora Fairclough	72	71	67	70	280	£15000
Corinne Dibnah	72	73	70	70	285	10150
Carin Hjalmarsson	72	71	71	72	286	7000
Karen Lunn	75	68	71	73	287	4380
Jane Geddes	73	74	71	69	287	4380
Annika Sorenstam	75	74	71	67	287	4380
Trish Johnson	73	73	72	70	288	3000
Mette Hageman	77	73	66	73	289	2500
Laura Davies	74	74	68	74	290	2240
Susan Moon	74	70	73	74	291	1853
Catrin Nilsmark	77	69	72	73	291	1853
Helen Alfredsson	74	76	71	70	291	1853

2 - 5 September
WATERFORD DAIRIES ENGLISH OPEN
THE TYTHERINGTON CLUB, MACCLESFIELD,
CHESHIRE, ENGLAND

Laura Davies	71	72	64	70	277	£9000
Marie-Laure de Lorenzi	67	70	71	70	278	6090
Debbie Petrizzi	71	74	70	71	286	4200
Corinne Dibnah	74	72	71	70	287	2892
Annika Sorenstam	71	72	72	72	287	2892
Laurette Maritz-Atkins	74	74	73	69	290	2100
Federica Dassu	74	73	71	73	291	1800
Debbie Dowling	74	72	77	69	292	1348
Trish Johnson	76	74	72	70	292	1348
Dale Reid	76	73	71	72	292	1348
Sofia Gronberg Whitmore	68	72	81	72	293	1068
Lisa Hackney	75	74	72	72	293	1068

16 - 19 September
BMW ITALIAN LADIES' OPEN
GOLF CLUB LIGNANO, LIGNANO SABBIADORO, ITALY

Amaya Arruti	67	65	68	70	270	£15750
Annika Sorenstam	67	70	68	67	272	10650
Kristal Parker	69	66	68	71	274	7350
Corinne Dibnah	69	68	76	65	278	5060
Anne Jones	71	63	76	68	278	5060
Lora Fairclough	71	69	68	72	280	3412
Helen Wadsworth	71	67	71	71	280	3412
Laura Davies	70	70	66	76	282	2487
Lisa Hackney	71	69	71	71	282	2487
Karine Espinasse	69	70	74	70	283	2015

Danielle Ammaccapane	69	74	69	71	283	2015
Sofia Gronberg Whitmore		69	70	74	71	284	1706
Laurette Maritz-Atkins	72	68	73	71	284	1706
Lisa DePaulo		69	71	73	71	284	1706

21 - 24 October
VAR FRENCH OPEN
STE. MAXIME & ST ENDREOL, THE VAR, FRANCE

Marie-Laure de Lorenzi	72	79	69	220	£9000
Federica Dassu	70	78	73	221	5145
Karina Orum	73	79	69	221	5145
Jane Hill	73	78	71	222	2628
Gillian Stewart	75	73	74	222	2628
Isabella Maconi	78	75	69	222	2628
Debbie Dowling	74	80	69	223	1800
Lora Fairclough	73	78	73	224	1500
Corinne Soules	75	76	74	225	1272
Debbie Petrizzi	77	75	73	225	1272
Catrin Nilsmark	75	75	76	226	1068
Muffin Spencer-Devlin	76	76	74	226	1068

Spain's Amaya Arruti won the Italian Open

Perfect timing: After a series of near misses, French favourite Marie-Laure de Lorenzi won the final event of the year... in France

1993 · WPG EUROPEAN TOUR MONEY LIST: TOP 50

#	Name	Amount	#	Name	Amount	#	Name	Amount
1	Karen Lunn	£81,266	18	Janet Soulsby	16,393	34	Valerie Michaud	10,365
2	Laura Davies	64,938	19	Karina Orum	15,841	35	Julie Forbes	9,605
3	Annika Sorenstam	55,927	20	Mette Hageman	15,664	36	Claire Duffy	9,235
4	Marie-Laure de Lorenzi	46,479	21	Susan Moon	14,450	37	Veronique Palli	9,197
5	Liselotte Neumann	39,530	22	Gillian Stewart	14,431	38	Allison Shapcott	8,856
6	Helen Dobson	38,179	23	Kristal Parker	13,735	39	Sarah Gautrey	8,799
7	Corinne Dibnah	34,429	24	Regine Lautens	13,682	40	Sally Prosser	8,281
8	Lora Fairclough	28,625	25	Helen Wadsworth	13,567	41	Caroline Hall	7,674
9	Federica Dassu	27,707	26	Debbie Petrizzi	13,365	42	Catherine Panton-Lewis	7,590
10	Dale Reid	25,553	27	Helen Alfredsson	13,116	43	Jane Hill	7,325
11	Mardi Lunn	23,495	28	Lisa Hackney	12,656	44	Xonia Wunsch-Ruiz	6,925
12	Laurette Maritz-Atkins	23,145	29	Shani Waugh	12581	45	Diane Barnard	6,455
13	Alison Nicholas	22,772	30	Karine Espinasse	11,565	46	Susan Shapcott	6,139
14	Catrin Nilsmark	21,052	31	Sofia Gronberg Whitmore	11,348	47	Karen Pearce	5,990
15	Carin Hjalmarsson	19,309	32	Debbie Dowling	11,295	48	Rae Hast	5,723
16	Amaya Arruti	18,579	33	Corinne Soules	10,689	49	Asa Gottmo	5,606
17	Trish Johnson	17,452				50	Anne Jones	5,521

1993 · TOUR WINNERS SUMMARY

KRP WORLD LADIES' CLASSIC	Karen Lunn (Aus)
FORD GOLF CLASSIC	Federica Dassu (It)
HOLIDAY INN LEIDEN OPEN	Corinne Dibnah (Aus)
BMW EUROPEAN MASTERS	Helen Dobson (GB)
HENNESSY LADIES' CUP	Liselotte Neumann (Swe)
THE EUROPEAN LADIES' CLASSIC	Mardi Lunn (Aus)
WEETABIX WOMEN'S BRITISH OPEN	Karen Lunn (Aus)
IBM LADIES' OPEN	Lora Fairclough (GB)
LADIES' ENGLISH OPEN	Laura Davies (GB)
ITALIAN LADIES' OPEN	Amaya Arruti (Sp)
VAR FRENCH OPEN	Marie-Laure de Lorenzi (Fr)

Frustrated by her poor form, Karen Lunn seriously contemplated giving up golf in 1992 – it's just as well she didn't!

Annika Sorenstam

EUROPEAN GOLFER OF THE YEAR

A Profile by Patricia Davies

At the end of 1993, there was an unexpected name at the top of the European Solheim Cup standings. Annika Sorenstam, a 23 year old Swede, who should really be a senior at the University of Arizona this year, instead started her second season as a professional out ahead of vastly more experienced campaigners such as Laura Davies, Trish Johnson and Alison Nicholas.

Sorenstam was Europe's Rookie of the Year in 1993 – as a reward Ford have given her the use of a new Mondeo in 1994 – and she is one of the reasons there is now such a buoyant mood about a Tour that has spent the last few years struggling to survive. She and other youngsters like Helen Dobson, Lora Fairclough and Amaya Arruti are helping the established stars to breathe life into women's golf everywhere, not just in Europe.

Sweden, of course, has established itself as a regular supplier of stars to the Tour, with Liselotte Neumann and Helen Alfredsson finding success at the highest level. Both have won major championships in America and they were unbeaten in the sensational Solheim Cup victory at Dalmahoy. They are thoroughly Americanised but that week in Scotland they astounded their US opponents – who thought they knew their Swedes – with the intensity of their play and the complexity of their language. And, of course, it was Catrin

Nilsmark, another Swede, unsung until then, who ensured her own little niche in golfing history by holing the winning putt. Sorenstam hopes to uphold that tradition.

'I would love to play at The Greenbrier,' she said. 'It's been a dream for the last couple of years and now that I've got some points, I want to keep that up. It would be so much fun to be in the team. I've spoken to Laura Davies about it and she was so pumped up – and that was in June last year! It's a huge event and to become a part of it would be awesome.'

Many good judges regard Sorenstam as moderately awesome herself. Pia Nilsson of the Swedish Golf Federation, who knows her well, rates her higly and Mickey Walker, the European Solheim Cup captain, who intends to get to know the young Swede better this season, has been very impressed so far.

'I know she works tremendously hard,' Walker said, 'and she's got a very good attitude on the course. She conducts herself in a manner any professional would like to. She's friendly without being over-the-top and she gets annoyed with herself on the course without it being detrimental to her game. She's incredibly motivated and wants to do everything as well as she can – to be the best it's possible to be. Pia walked round with Annika somewhere and said to her afterwards, 'That was great,' and Annika responded, 'Yes, but I want to know what I

could have done better'. She's always seeking improvement and that's wonderful.'

The Sorenstam game is not a power game in the Laura Davies mould – the Swede is too slight to compete on that level – yet she is, as Walker puts it, 'sneaky impressive'. 'You're not in awe of the shots she hits, the way you're in awe of Laura's. Annika doesn't hit the ball phenomenal distances but her strength is that she has no weaknesses. Every department is solid. You can't imagine her hitting horrible shots. She's so steady and seems to be incredibly mature. She realises there's no predestined rate of performance in golf and will continue to work and work to achieve what she wants.'

Perhaps the only thing that surprised anyone about Sorenstam last year was that she did not win, an expectation which showed just how highly she was regarded. Her record as an amateur was outstanding and included a victory in the NCAA Championship, the premier American college tournament. She was also the leading individual player in the Espirto Santo, the Women's World Amateur Team Championship, in Vancouver in 1992 and that same year reached the final of the US Amateur Championship, losing by one hole to her great rival Vicki Goetze.

The American player has now also turned professional and Sorenstam was looking forward to meeting up with her again. 'It'll be fun', she enthused. But her memories of their 1992 final were not so rosy. 'I'll never forget it,' she said, grimacing at the thought of the shot that lost her a chance of the title. 'We were all-square playing the last and I made a big mistake with my second shot. The green was over water with the flag in a tricky place and I made the fastest

swing I've ever made in my whole life. It was awful.' 'Splash' went the ball and splash went her chances of becoming the first Swede to win the US Amateur.

She is by nature a fast swinger and one of the refreshing things about her is that she takes so little time to play her shots; there is none of the endless fiddling and fussing that most professionals seem to regard as imperative. 'I don't think there's anything to think about once the club is chosen and in your hand. I hate to wait.'

However, there will inevitably be plenty of waiting in her professional career and it is as well that Sorenstam learned the value of patience a while ago. 'I grew into it,' she explained, having admitted to being a bit of a club-thrower in her youth. 'Someone at the club told me I was behaving childishly and that I couldn't play if I didn't change. I didn't have a choice. Then I noticed that with self-control I played better and then I started to become really consistent.'

That consistency has become her great strength. She finished runner-up four times in Europe last season and was fourth in the Standard Register Ping tournament at Moon Valley in Phoenix – after initially being denied access by an over-zealous official who refused to believe she was a player. He should know different now.

The performance in Arizona, familiar territory to her from her years at college (she studied nutrition but did not graduate) alerted everyone to her potential and she did not disappoint on her first outing on the European Tour. Leading after 54 holes, she finished second to Federica Dassu in the Ford Classic and conducted herself with such aplomb that no-one doubted a star was in the making. 'She'll win sooner rather than later,' Walker forecast.

Everything did not run totally smoothly in 1993, however, for late in the year Sorenstam narrowly failed to win her 1994 LPGA Tour card and had to settle for a conditional card. 'It was frustrating,' she said, 'I felt really prepared beforehand, both mentally and golfwise, but I got nervous

She won the NCAA Championship last year but has decided not to return to America for the time being. She has not turned professional yet but if and when she decides to do so, she will find her sister on hand to help.

'We used to be tough on each other,'

when it started. Everyone was so fired up; the course was long and I didn't start too well and then I was thinking constantly about what I needed to score to qualify. It's something I never want to do again.'

It will be a major shock if she ever needs to, for she is level-headed, eager to learn and has more than enough ability. She also has the perfect incentive to keep on improving : a younger sister, Charlotta, who is also proving to be outstandingly talented.

Annika said, 'but not any more. We help each other and share experiences. We can talk about competition and I just want her to play as well as she can. Temperamentally, she's calmer than I am and more laid-back. I'm always on the go.'

Sorenstam used to put all her energies into tennis, being one of the millions of Swedes attracted to the racquet by Bjorn Borg, but was, she said, burned out by the age of 16. Golf should be grateful.

Amateur Golf in Europe

With it being an 'odd year' there was no Curtis Cup to play for in 1993 – although there was certainly one to prepare for – and no Espirito Santo Trophy either (the next staging of the biennial World Amateur Team Championships will be in France in September (see page 117).

The above is not intended to suggest that patriotism was somehow put into mothballs in 1993; the calendar still contained several important international matches, but individual performances inevitably stood out a little more last season, and there were two that were precisely that – outstanding.

Among those players most likely to be representing Great Britain and Ireland in the 1994 Curtis Cup at Chattanooga, Julie Hall of England and Catriona Lambert of Scotland were easily the most successful. Lambert captured the major prize, the British Amateur Championship at Royal

(Left) Julie Hall, winner of the British Ladies Strokeplay Championship; (right) Sweden's Charlotta Sorenstam

Lytham (see page 108) and Hall, a winner of that championship in 1990, took the British Strokeplay title at Gullane. Both players collected three further domestic titles and Lambert also won the Spanish Amateur Championship at San Roque. Writing in *Women & Golf* magazine last

however, and the European Amateur Championship in Torino proved that the present crop of British golfers is far from invincible. Although there was a strong British contingent present in Italy, the best placed among their number at the end of the week turned out to be defending

Scotland's 'big three':
Catriona Lambert,
Janice Moodie and
Mhairi McKay

December, Lewine Mair commented, 'If the women's amateur game boasted the equivalent of the professional world's Ping Leaderboard, Catriona Lambert and Julie Hall would surely feature in the top three.'

As for talk of a 'big three', Scottish golf can currently boast one of its own with Janice Moody and Mhairi McKay (the British Girls Champion) strongly tipped to join Lambert in the select eight bound for Chattanooga. And with the 1994 Curtis Cup in mind, there was one very significant biennial amateur team match held in Europe in September 1993: Great Britain & Ireland versus the Continent of Europe for the Vagliano Trophy. Hall, Lambert, Moody and McKay were all members of the Great Britain & Ireland team that retained the cup (winning 13½ – 10½) at Morfontaine.

Complacency must not be encouraged,

champion Joanne Morley (who has since turned professional) and Nicola Buxton – they tied for 11th. The winner was Vibeke Stensrud from Norway who compiled impressive scores of 71-67-70-69 (11 under par) to win by four strokes.

Finishing fifth in that European Amateur Championship was Sweden's Charlotta Sorenstam, sister of WPG European Tour star Annika Sorenstam. In 1993 Charlotta emulated her sister's individual triumph in America's NCAA Championships, the premier US college event. Several other European amateurs made an impression in America last year, among whom were Britain's Lisa Walton (a San Jose University team-mate of Vibeke Stensrud), Estefania Knuth of Spain and Denmark's Iben Tinning; the latter both reached the quarter-finals of the 1993 US Amateur Championship.

British Women's Amateur Championship

In 1893 the first British Ladies' Championship was staged at St Anne's on the Lancashire coast. In keeping with the spirit of the age the winner was the very British, Lady Margaret Scott. One hundred years later – and in keeping with the spirit of a new age – the now-called Women's Amateur Championship had become very European. The previous two winners, in 1991 and 1992, were Valerie Michaud of France and Pernille Pedersen of Denmark. 1993's event maybe remembered as 'the year the clock turned back'.

Last August the championship returned to Lancashire, to the rugged, uncompromising links of Royal Lytham. French and Danish golfers again   played an important part in the proceedings but by the end it became a very British affair, and the winner of the 1993 Amateur Championship, though not a Lady Scott, was nonetheless a Scottish lady.

Few things add more to a championship than a local player exceeding expectations. Kirsty Speak from nearby Clitheroe was acknowledged as a fine golfer but it is doubtful that even she could have imagined quite how well she would perform at Royal Lytham.

In the first round Speak defeated French player Cecilia Mourgue D'Algue and in the third round beat her daughter, Kristel D'Algue. In between times she ended the hopes of the defending champion, crushing Pedersen by an impressive 6 & 4 margin. The legendary Mary McKenna became her

quarter-final victim and in the semi-finals she gained a superb triumph over Julie Hall.

In the other half of the draw Catriona Lambert also defeated players from France and Denmark and in the first round won a tough contest with Mhairi McKay. Lambert was forced to come from behind in each of these games and her battling instincts were again required when she went three down after five in her semi-final with England's Sandy Lambert. But Catriona eventually won the match at the first extra hole.

So to the final. There was no doubt who was the underdog; nor was there any doubting the crowd's favourite. The local 'Lancashire lass' went one up after eight. Could she pull off a shock victory? She had played superbly all week... but then Lambert had been playing superbly all year. Eight holes later it was all over. The famous trophy was heading north towards Scotland.

June 8 - 12
1993 WOMEN'S AMATEUR CHAMPIONSHIP
ROYAL LYTHAM, LANCASHIRE, ENGLAND

QUARTER-FINALS:
C Lambert beat I Tinning 2 & 1
K Speak beat M McKenna 4 & 3
S Lambert beat K McKenna 2 & 1
J Hall beat J Moodie 2 & 1

SEMI-FINALS:
C Lambert beat S Lambert at 19th
K Speak beat J Hall 2 & 1

FINAL
C LAMBERT beat K SPEAK 3 & 2

· ROLL OF HONOUR ·

1893	Lady Margaret Scott	1934	Helen Holm	1977	Angela Uzielli
1894	Lady Margaret Scott	1935	Wanda Morgan	1978	Edwina Kennedy (Aus)
1895	Lady Margaret Scott	1936	Pam Barton	1979	Maureen Madill
1896	Amy Pascoe	1937	Jessie Anderson	1980	Anne Quast Sander (USA)
1897	Edith O Orr	1938	Helen Holm	1981	Belle Robertson
1898	Miss L Thomson	1939	Pam Barton	1982	Kitrina Douglas
1899	May Hezlet	1940	No competition	1983	Jill Thornhill
1900	Rhona Adair	1941	No competition	1984	Jody Rosenthal (USA)
1901	Miss Graham	1942-5	No competition	1985	Lillian Behan (Ire)
1902	May Hezlet	1946	Jean Hetherington	1986	Marnie McGuire (NZ)
1903	Rhona Adair	1947	Babe Zaharias (USA)	1987	Janet Collingham
1904	Lottie Dod	1948	Louise Suggs (USA)	1988	Joanne Furby
1905	Miss B Thompson	1949	Frances Stephens	1989	Helen Dobson
1906	Mrs Kennion	1950	Vicomtesse de St Sauveur (Fr)	1990	Julie Hall
1907	May Hezlet	1951	Mrs P G MacCann	1991	Valerie Michaud (Fr)
1908	Miss M Titterton	1952	Moira Paterson	1992	Pernille Pedersen (Den)
1909	Dorothy Campbell	1953	Marlene Stewart (Can)	1993	Catriona Lambert
1910	Grant Suttie	1954	Frances Stephens		
1911	Dorothy Campbell	1955	Jessie Anderson Valentine		
1912	Gladys Ravenscroft	1956	Margaret Smith		
1913	Muriel Dodd	1957	Philomena Garvey		
1914	Cecil Leitch	1958	Jessie Anderson Valentine		
1915	No competition	1959	Elizabeth Price		
1916	No competition	1960	Barabara McIntire (USA)		
1917-8	No competition	1961	Marley Spearman		
1919	No competition	1962	Marley Spearman		
1920	Cecil Leitch	1963	Brigitte Varangot (Fr)		
1921	Cecil Leitch	1964	Carol Sorenson (USA)		
1922	Joyce Wethered	1965	Brigitte Varangot (Fr)		
1923	Doris Chambers	1966	Elizabeth Chadwick		
1924	Joyce Wethered	1967	Elizabeth Chadwick		
1925	Joyce Wethered	1968	Brigitte Varangot (Fr)		
1926	Cecil Leitch	1969	Catherine Lacoste (Fr)		
1927	Thion de la Chaume (Fr)	1970	Dinah Oxley		
1928	Nanette Le Blan (Fr)	1971	Mickey Walker		
1929	Joyce Wethered	1972	Mickey Walker		
1930	Diana Fishwick	1973	Ann Irvin		
1931	Enid Wilson	1974	Carol Semple (USA)		
1932	Enid Wilson	1975	Nancy Syms (USA)		
1933	Enid Wilson	1976	Cathy Panton		

Catriona Lambert

The Rest of the World

5

Asia and Australia

Researched by Bill Johnson

Sally Prosser

Laura Davies is on record as saying that her goal each year is to win a tournament in Europe and a tournament in America. In 1993 she achieved her ambition but, in addition, she also won in Asia (in January) and in Australia (in December). Her victory in the first event of the 1993 Kosaido Asia Circuit – the Thailand Open at the luxurious Panya Resort near Pattaya – was the opening salvo that would see British golfers go on to dominate the five week tour.

The former British and US Women's Open champion had to produce a birdie at the second play-off hole against Australian Karen Lunn to seal her victory in Thailand after rounds of 74-71-68 had left her in a deadlock with the Sydney golfer. (A week earlier Lunn had beaten Sandrine Mendiburu in a play-off to win the KRP World Classic in Kuala Lumpur, the first event of the European Tour).

Soon after her triumph, Davies left for America and it was her fellow British golfers, Sally Prosser and Janet Soulsby who benefited most from her absence. Both achieved maiden professional victories and indeed both won their respective events – Soulsby the Singapore Open at Tanah Merah and Prosser the Malaysian Open at Rahmen Putra – by the impressive margin of six strokes.

Prosser was undoubtedly the star of the '93 circuit for in addition to her win in Malaysia, the feature of which was a brilliant course-record 64, she finished in the top six in all five Asian events and comfortably headed the Order of Merit table. The American Kim Lasken and Japan's Fusako Nagato were the tour's other two winners, Lasken defying a tropical storm to win in Indonesia and Nagato capturing the tour's final event, the Republic of China Open at Chang Gung in Taipei.

Royal Pines sounds a world away from Chang Gung and it was here, on Australia's Gold Coast in December that Davies defeated an international field to clinch her fourth title in 1993 and the 25th victory of her career.

The Alpine Australian Masters was the only women's professional event ' Down Under' last year but the amateur scene was as busy as ever and the Australian Ladies Amateur Championship produced a home winner when 23 year-old Anne-Marie Knight from South Australia beat New Zealand's Gina Scott in an exciting 36 hole final at Indooroopilly.

1993 · LADIES' ASIAN TOUR

21 - 23 January
THAILAND OPEN

L Davies (GB)	74	71	68	213
K Lunn (Aus)	71	73	69	213
(Davies won play-off)				
S Prosser (GB)	74	77	68	219
C Dibnah (Aus)	72	77	70	219
W Doolan (Aus)	74	72	73	219

28 - 30 January
INDONESIAN OPEN

K Lasken (US)	71	76	147
L Fairclough (GB)	76	73	149
C Hjalmarsson (Swe)	76	74	150
L Hackney (GB)	77	74	151
L DePaulo (US)	76	75	151

4 - 6 February
SINGAPORE OPEN

J Soulsby (GB)	76	69	68	213
W Doolan (Aus)	72	75	72	219
H Wadsworth (GB)	75	73	72	220
L Sugg (US)	76	68	76	220
H Dobson (GB)	75	70	75	220

11 - 13 February
MALAYSIAN OPEN

S Prosser (GB)	64	71	75	210
H Wadsworth (GB)	72	72	72	216
M Bertilskold (Swe)	72	71	73	216
X Wunsch (Sp)	74	71	72	217
M Lunn (Aus)	71	75	72	218

18 - 20 February
REPUBLIC OF CHINA OPEN

F Nagata (Jap)	68	73	69	210
J Figley (US)	71	71	70	212
S Prosser (GB)	71	72	70	213
N Kessler (US)	72	73	69	214

KOSAIDO ORDER OF MERIT

Winner:	S Prosser (GB)	338 pts
Runner-up:	J Soulsby (GB)	274

1993 · AUSTRALIAN MASTERS

10 -12 December
ALPINE AUSTRALIAN MASTERS
ROYAL PINES, QUEENSLAND

L Davies	68	74	69	211	$A37500
L A Mills	72	72	68	212	17500
J Geddes	73	66	73	212	17500
M Spencer-Devlin	67	72	73	212	17500
L Wen-Lin	69	74	70	213	10000
J Sevil	75	71	68	214	9000
C Dibnah	72	70	72	214	9000
J Crafter	70	72	73	215	6250
A Sorenstam	69	73	73	215	6250
K Webb	71	69	75	215	(Am)
K Tschetter	74	68	73	215	6250
C Figg-Currier	71	69	75	215	6250
S Gautrey	72	74	70	216	4250
A Munt	74	71	71	216	4250
E Orley	71	72	74	217	3600
J Higgins	71	72	74	217	3600
K Lunn	77	70	71	218	3150
D Reid	74	71	73	218	3150
S Daniels	70	73	75	218	3150
L Neumann	72	74	73	219	2850

Laura Davies

1993 AUSTRALIAN LADIES AMATEUR
FINAL: Anne-Marie Knight beat Gina Scott (2 up)

Japanese Tour Review

By 'Duke' Ishikawa

It was a great year of firsts in Japan. For several young players on the Japanese LPGA Tour 1993 will be remembered as the season when they made their big breakthrough. It was also the year when the 'Yokozuna' or 'Grand Champion' of ladies golf in Japan, Ayako Okamoto finally won her first Japanese National Open Championship.

Despite this long overdue victory in her country's premier event, Okamoto had mixed fortunes in 1993. The first half of her year was spent in America where she played poorly and was overshadowed by fellow Japanese golfer, Hiromi Kobayashi who won twice on the LPGA Tour. Okamoto started her Japanese campaign well enough, for in addition to winning the Japan Open in late June she claimed the Ito-en title in August, but later in the season she threw away a number of winning opportunities. These lapses were very uncharacteristic (although they were strangely mirrored on the men's tour by her great counterpart, Jumbo Ozaki) and many Japanese writers began to question whether, at 42 years of age, Okamoto's powers, especially her great putting touch, were beginning to decline.

In addition to the ups and downs of Okamoto, another feature of 1993, and a major reason for the proliferation of first time winners, was the limited success of overseas players. Last year only six of the 37 Japanese LPGA events were won by non-Japanese golfers; in 1992 the number was 14. There were important wins for Lotte Neumann (in the Takara event) and Betsy King (Toray Japan Cup) and a surprise play-off victory for New Zealander Sheree Higgins (Fuji-Sankei) but the Korean and Taiwanese golfers proved to be much less of

Three victories helped Mayumi Hirase to claim number one position on the Japanese LPGA Order of Merit

Ayako Okamoto won two tournaments in Japan in 1993, including, for the first time, the Japanese National Open

a force than they had been in recent seasons.

The Japanese Tour always commences in the far south of the country - where it is considerably warmer in March! - and the year got off to a surprise beginning with the first four tournaments being shared by the unheralded pair of Fuki Kido and Kumiko Hiyoshi.

Perhaps the biggest impressions in 1993 were made by two 25 year-olds, Michiko Hattori and Toshimi Kimura, and by 27 year-old Kaori Harada who won the prestigious Japanese LPGA Championship as well as the final event of the season, the Meiji Cup, where she capitalised on an extraordinary late collapse by Okamoto.

Until last year Hattori was best known for winning the 1985 US Women's Amateur Championship while still a student. A week after the Japan Open she claimed her first 'home victory' in the Mizuno event and the manner in which she then added two more titles before the end of the season suggested

that she could be the player to beat in 1994.

The long-hitting Kimura also made her breakthrough in 1993 when she won the Mitsukoshi Cup in early April and, like Hattori, went on to win three times. Kimura eventually finished second on the money list and Hattori was fourth. For much of the season, however, the battle for the number one position was contested by Mayumi Murai and Mayumi Hirase.

Murai enjoyed a sensational run of form during the summer when in the space of seven weeks she won three tournament and lost a play-off to Okamoto in the Japan Open. But Hirase, who had missed much of the 1992 season through being in hospital, was easily the most consistent performer on the Tour in 1993. She triumphed in the World Ladies tournament in May; captured the Junon tournament in July and, following a sequence of top finishes throughout the summer, won the Fujitsu tournament in October to clinch the number one spot.

1993 · JAPAN LPGA TOUR ·

25 year-old Michiko Hattori is being widely tipped as the next great Japanese golfer

ORDER OF MERIT: TOP 25

1	Mayumi Hirase	Yen 81,474,399
2	Toshimi Kimura	67,780,200
3	Mayumi Murai	64,970,541
4	Michiko Hattori	60,703,553
5	Kumiko Hiyoshi	53,919,706
6	Kaori Harada	46,830,545
7	Aiko Takasu	44,725,960
8	Fuki Kido	43,560,566
9	Ayako Okamoto	41,035,953
10	Nayoko Yoshikawa	39,376,888
11	Ok-Hee Ku (Korea)	38,848,996
12	Kaori Higo	38,805,830
13	Chieko Nishida	38,473,627
14	Yuko Moriguchi	35,447,083
15	Ai-Yu Tu (Taiwan)	34,043,478
16	Fusako Nagata	32,631,142
17	Junko Yasui	32,463,869
18	Miyuki Shimabukuro	30,165,626
19	Akiko Fukushima	27,590,197
20	Suzuko Maeda	27,582,037
21	Ikuyo Shiotani	26,971,366
22	Chaco Higuchi	26,092,655
23	Akane Ohshiro	24,911,358
24	Atsuko Hikage	24,503,083
25	Aiko Hashimoto	24,245,825

TOURNAMENT WINNERS

Daikin	Fuki Kido
Chiyoda	Kumiko Hiyoshi
Saishunkan	Fuki Kido
Kibun	Kumiko Hiyoshi
Tohato	Ai-Yu Tu (Taiwan)
Mitsukoshi	Toshimi Kimura
Yonex	Aiko Takasu
Nasuogawa	Chikayo Yamazaki
Katokichi	Toshimi Kimura
World Ladies	Mayumi Hirase
Yakult	Aiko Takasu
Chukyo TV	Chieko Nishida
Toto	Mayumi Murai
Mitsubishi	Bie-Shyun Huang (Taiwan)
Suntory	Suzuko Maeda
Dunlop	Mayumi Murai
Japan's National Open	Ayako Okamoto
Mizuno	Michiko Hattori
Toyo	Mayumi Murai
Resort Trust	Miyuki Shimabukuro
Junon	Mayumi Hirase
Stanley	Yuko Moriguchi
NEC	Mitsuko Hirata
Ito-en	Ayako Okamoto
KTV	Atsuko Hikage
Fuji-Sankei	S Higgins (NZ)
Japan LPGA Championship	Kaori Harada
Asahi	Kayo Mochizuki
Miyagi TV	Fusako Nagata
Tokai	Michiko Hattori
Takara	L Neumann (Swe)
Fujitsu	Mayumi Hirase
Itsuki	Ok-Hee Ku (Korea)
Nichirei (team)	US beat Japan
Toray Japan Queens	B King (US)
Itoki	Michiko Hattori
Elleair	Toshimi Kimura
Meiji Cup	Kaori Harada

The World Amateur Team Championship

(FOR THE ESPIRITO SANTO TROPHY)

· ROLL OF HONOUR ·

YEAR	VENUE	WINNER
1964	St Germain, France	France 588
1966	Mexico City CC	Unites States 580
1968	Victoria GC, Australia	United States 616
1970	Club de Campo, Spain	United States 598
1972	Hindu CC, Argentina	United States 583
1974	Campo de Golf, Dominica	United States 620
1976	Vilamoura, Portugal	United States 605
1978	Pacific Harbour, Fiji	Australia 596
1980	Pinehurst No 2, USA	United States 588
1982	Geneva, Switzerland	United States 579
1984	Royal Hong Kong	United States 585
1986	Caracas, Venezuela	Spain 580
1988	Drottingholm, Sweden	United States 587
1990	Christchurch, New Zealand	United States 585
1992	Vancouver, Canada	Spain 588

The spectacular French National GC near Paris is where Spain will defend the biennial World Amateur Team Championship trophy in September

6

1994
An Eventful Season

January

Towards the sun. England's — better make that Yorkshire's — Alison Nicholas strikes an iron shot from the fairway and brings us into the New Year.

With Europe in the grip of midwinter, and America's LPGA Tour not commencing until February, South East Asia becomes the focus for professional golf in January. The four-week Asian Circuit begins in Bangkok where Laura Davies will be seeking to emulate her victory in the 1993 Thailand Open.

A week later comes the Malaysian Open in Penang followed by the Indonesian Open. Meanwhile, many of the world's top women amateurs journey to Florida to play on the popular Orange Blossom Tour where the events comprise a refreshing mix of fourball, strokeplay and matchplay golf.

February

Back into the shadows.

America's Betsy King — Leading Moneywinner on the 1993 LPGA Tour — putts across a green that is dappled in sunlight.

The Healthsouth Palm Beach Classic at Lake Worth is the LPGA Tour's opening event of 1994. Betsy King will be anxious to secure an early victory and so capture her 30th title - and, more significantly, gain her passport to the LPGA Hall of Fame. Tammie Green will be the defending champion in Florida and two weeks later Canadian Lisa Walters will be seeking a third successive victory in the Hawaiian Open. The final event of the Asian Circuit takes place at the beginning of the month with the Republic of China Open at the wonderfully named Chang Gung Golf Club in Taipei.

March

Beautiful but intimidating. The par four 6th hole at the Mission Hills Country Club near Palm Springs, home of the Dinah Shore tournament.

The Dinah Shore is the year's first Major championship and it takes place at the end of a very action-packed month on the LPGA Tour. Prior to Helen Alfredsson's defence of that title, there is the inaugural LPGA Tournament of Champions at Grand Cypress, Orlando; then comes the 'Arizona double' with the Ping/Welch's Championship in Tucson, followed by the Standard Register Ping tournament at the Moon Valley Country Club in Phoenix — scene of Patty Sheehan's great 'Hall of Fame victory' in 1993. March also heralds the beginning of the 1994 Japanese LPGA Tour, with Mayumi Hirase defending her Leading Moneywinners crown.

April

From palms to pines.
The Duchess Course at Woburn adds a new dimension to
the phrase 'a tree-lined golf course'.

In the third week of April the Duchess Course will once again host the Ford Classic, the opening event of the 1994 WPG European Tour. Pictured above (driving-off) is Annika Sorenstam who finished runner-up to Federica Dassu in 1993's event - no mean feat given that this was the Swedish golfer's professional debut in Europe. After a three week break the LPGA Tour resumes its schedule with the Atlanta Women's Championship at Eagle's Landing, followed by the Sprint Championship at Indigo Lakes, Daytona Beach: Trish Johnson defends the former and Kristi Albers the latter.

May

Patty Sheehan will be looking to increase her tally of Grandslam titles when she defends the now McDonald's sponsored LPGA Championship in May.

Hosted by the du Pont Country Club, Wilmington, Delaware, the LPGA Championship is easily the month's most important event in America. In addition to a place in history it rewards the winner with a huge cheque at the end of the week; it is conceivable, however, that a player might accumulate even greater riches by 'cleaning up' in the JC Penney/LPGA Skins Game in Texas. Betsy King won that event in 1993 — surprisingly, it was her only victory in America last year (although she did win an LPGA tournament in Japan at the end of the season). On the other side of the Atlantic, the WPG European Tour travels to Portugal for the Costa Azul Ladies' Classic.

June

There are water hazards and there are water hazards...
breathtaking views of Lake Geneva may prove distracting when
the WPG European Tour visits majestic Royal Club Evian.

The first Evian Masters tournament promises to be (in every sense) an extremely attractive addition to the WPG European Tour calendar. With total prize money surpassed only by the Weetabix British Open, and a magnificent location on the French/Swiss border, a quality field is assured. Golf in Europe certainly gathers momentum in June for, immediately following the Evian Masters, there is another new tournament in Austria and the BMW European Masters in Belgium. In America the LPGA Tour moves from Michigan to Minnesota then from New York to New Jersey. The Japanese Open Championship is traditionally held in June and in the amateur game, Newport Golf Club in Wales is the venue for the British Women's Amateur Championship.

July

The Curtis Cup charge:
will the euphoric scenes be repeated in Chattanooga?
And will Lauri Merten retain her US Open crown?

Eight of the best amateurs from Great Britain and Ireland will be defending the trophy they won on the final green of the final match at Hoylake... and eight of the best amateurs from America will be trying their best to stop them. Just a few days before the 28th Curtis Cup encounter, the Indianwood Golf Club at Lake Orion, Michigan is the venue for the 49th US Women's Open. Betsy King won the championship when it was held over this same course in 1989. July also brings the US Women's Amateur Championship. Back in the Old World, there are three WPG European Tour events: the Hennessey Cup, the European Classic and the Ford Irish Open.

August

Where Tours converge: leading players from both sides of the Atlantic will be at Woburn in mid-August to contest the Weetabix Women's British Open Championship...

... and they will all be trying to prevent Karen Lunn – a golfer from 'Down Under' – from retaining her title. It is several years since the Weetabix British Open established itself as the most prestigious professional tournament in Europe; from 1994 it also becomes one of the major events of the LPGA Tour. One week before the British Open, Dalmahoy stages yet another new European tournament, the Scottish Open. The biggest event in North America during August is the du Maurier Classic at the Ottawa Hunt Club in Ontario, Canada: Brandie Burton is the reigning champion.

September

Laura Davies is likely to be challenging for a third successive victory in the English Open at Tytherington.

1993's English Open developed into a superb head-to-head matchplay-style confrontation between Davies (who won the event in 1992 by seven strokes) and a rejuvenated Marie-Laure de Lorenzi. There is a very international feel to golf in Europe during September with professional tournaments also taking place in the Netherlands, Italy and Spain. In France, The National GC near Paris hosts the biennial World Amateur Team Championship.

October

*USA v Europe: The Greenbrier will be the focus
of world attention when it stages the 3rd Solheim Cup match
in the third week of October.*

Notwithstanding Europe's spectacular success at Dalmahoy in 1992, JoAnne Carner's team will almost certainly begin as favourites to move one ahead in the series. Home advantage could prove crucial — as indeed it has on both previous occasions — although in her Foreword to this book the American Captain states her belief that the design of the Greenbrier course will not necessarily favour one side or the other. It should prove to be a fascinating contest, and perhaps the only thing we can be sure of is that both sides will be well prepared and extraordinarily determined... may the best team win!

November

The perfect finish for Japanese golfer, Hiromi Kobayashi:
East meets West in November as the LPGA Tour completes its
schedule with an event in Japan.

Betsy King has become something of a specialist at achieving end-of-season victories in Japan. Her triumph in the 1993 Toray Japan Queens Cup enabled the American to scoop most of the LPGA Tour's annual awards. Kobayashi won twice in the US last year and she can be expected to lead a powerful home challenge. As for the Japanese LPGA Tour, it continues through to the end of the month with the Meiji Cup, a 'tournament of champions' style event, providing a grand finale to the 1994 season.

December

From Japan to Australia: the Japanese-designed
Royal Pines Golf Club in Queensland is the home of
the Australian Ladies' Masters.

Royal Pines is among the brightest of several golfing jewels on the Gold Coast. In December it stages the Australian Ladies' Masters - the only major ladies' professional tournament 'Down Under' — but an event that seems to be gaining in stature each year.

Laura Davies defeated a strong international field to win in 1993, her 25th success world-wide. And what of life after Royal Pines? It is almost Christmas and that means time to relax... and time to reflect on all those missed three-footers.

1994 Majors

A Preview by Matthew Chancellor

Bobby Jones, the great American gentleman amateur, stressed the importance of the major championships perfectly. 'There are,' said Jones, 'tournament winners, and *major* tournament winners.'

History judges its great players according to their performances in the 'Major' championships. As Nick Faldo plans his season around the Masters, the US Open, the British Open and the USPGA Championship, so the likes of Patty Sheehan and Betsy King start each new year with their own 'Major' ambitions.

Currently the women's Grand Slam is made up of the Nabisco Dinah Shore, the McDonald's LPGA Championship, the US Women's Open, and the du Maurier Ltd Classic. The status of the oldest two tournaments, the US Open and LPGA Championship is assured. But in the case of the Dinah Shore and the du Maurier, major status has been 'awarded' by the LPGA Tour in America within the last 15 years. Indeed, up until 1966, the now defunct Western Open and the Titleholders were regarded as major championships.

To an extent the major championships in women's golf are still evolving. And this year sees the strongest challenge yet by the Weetabix Women's British Open to be recognised as a 'Major' or Grand Slam tournament. First played in 1976, this year the Women's British Open will not only be the most important event in Europe but will be, for the first time, a fully-sanctioned LPGA Tour event.

The first women's major of the season, the Nabisco Dinah Shore (March 24-27) encourages the idea that it is the female equivalent of the Masters. An important similarity is that its field is made up of invited players.

First played in 1972, it was not until 1983 that the LPGA Tour awarded the Dinah Shore 'major' status. Ignoring the slightly absurd notion that major status can be given, the Dinah Shore does have a very special atmosphere and a tradition that secures its unique place in the women's game. As a twice winner of the title Betsy King pointed out after her second victory in 1990: 'It's hard to just designate a tournament a major, but this one has grown in stature over the years, the course has improved every year, and it has developed into a great tournament.'

Indeed, unlike the three other LPGA majors, the Dinah Shore is the only one to be played over the same course each year — the spectacular Mission Hills layout at Rancho Mirage in California. The tournament's special flavour owes much to the presence of the celebrity Dinah Shore herself, who always attends the tournament and presents the prize to the winner.

Majestic Mission Hills — home of the Dinah Shore tournament

The LPGA Championship (May 12-15) which this year celebrates its 40th anniversary, is the second oldest major in the women's game.

It was first held in 1955, when it was contested, for one year only, as a matchplay tournament. The first winner was Beverley

Helen Alfredsson and Dinah Shore pose with one of the most coveted trophies in ladies' golf

Hanson who defeated Louise Suggs 4&3 in the final. The following year it changed to strokeplay.

This year reveals a new chapter for the LPGA, with fast food giant McDonald's replacing car makers Mazda as title sponsor. To mark the occasion, McDonald's has increased the total prize money by $100,000 to a massive $1,100,000.

The championship will also be held for the first time at the Du Pont Country Club, Wilmington in Delaware, designed by Alfred Tull and William Gordon. The course is not new to the LPGA Tour: last year it hosted the McDonald's Championship won by Britain's Laura Davies. However, despite winning a tournament called McDonald's at a course called Du Pont over the same May weekend, it will be three-time LPGA champion Patty Sheehan, and not Davies, who is the defending champion.

Amid the slight uncertainty as to what properly constitutes a Grand Slam event one thing remains clear – the US Women's Open (July 21-24) is the most important championship in women's golf.

The oldest of the four LPGA majors, it was first played in 1946. It has a distinguished roll call of past champions, linking Sheehan, King and Pat Bradley in the modern age with the great names of the past, such as Patty Berg, Babe Zaharias, Louise Suggs and Mickey Wright. The championship is regularly played on genuinely great courses, including, over the years, Winged Foot, Baltusrol, Hazeltine, Colonial and Oakmont.

This year the tradition continues when the championship returns to Indianwood Golf Club, Lake Orion, Michigan, scene of the first of King's back-to-back US Open titles in 1989. Five years ago the course made an impact for the heather-like grass lining the fairways, which gave it the appearance of a Scottish links. Appearances

The champion and her cup: Lauri Merten (pictured during last season's McDonald's Championship) will defend her US Open crown at Indianwood

can be deceptive, however, and in truth Indianwood's high unmanageable rough was more in keeping with the men's US Open, than a British Open-type course.

Notwithstanding the impressive roll of honour, the most prestigious title in women's golf has eluded at least two of the game's greatest players. Kathy Whitworth, who holds the record for the most titles won on the LPGA Tour – an incredible 88 – found, like Sam Snead, that the US Open remained elusive. Today, Nancy Lopez, whom many credit with precipitating the massive injection of money into women's golf during the late '70s and early '80s, has also, so far, missed out on the US Open.

Lopez, 37 this year, no longer has time on her side if she is to claim that elusive prize. And were she to win at Indianwood, there would be no more popular champion.

Sandwiched between the US Women's Open and the final LPGA major of the year (the du Maurier Ltd Classic) is the only European 'major', the Weetabix Women's

British Open at Woburn, near Milton Keynes, England (August 11-14).

In 1994, for the first time in its 18-year history, the Women's British Open has become a recognised stop on the LPGA Tour. The significance of this move should not be underestimated. In previous years the LPGA Tour sanctioned releases to only four of its players to compete in the tournament, thus depriving it of a strong American presence. This year the field is expected to comprise 50 exempt players from the LPGA Money List, plus the top 50 players in Europe, making it the most truly international field in women's golf.

While the exact status of the tournament will probably only be determined as it becomes more established on the US circuit, at least two past American winners of the title, Sheehan and Jane Geddes, are enthusiastic that one day it will be universally recognised as a major. Says Geddes: 'The golf course is superb (it has

Former champions, England's Laura Davies and Australian Corinne Dibnah, can be expected to challenge strongly when the Weetabix British Open returns to Woburn in August

been held at Woburn each year since 1990), the spectators so knowledgeable, the organisation and the whole atmosphere could not be bettered. It is marvellous to be there. The title is right and it will surely become a major in world women's golf.'

The fourth LPGA major of the season is the du Maurier Ltd Classic (August 25-28).

The du Maurier is arguably the least celebrated of the women's majors. Perhaps the principal reason for this is that the event has undergone three name changes – originally La Canadienne, it became the

How many Majors will Brandie Burton win in the next ten years? Her first Grand Slam success came at last year's du Maurier Classic

Peter Jackson Classic from 1974 to 1982, before it acquired its current title.

In recent times, however, the tournament has lacked nothing a truly major-calibre winner couldn't put right. And that's just what it got a year ago when Brandie Burton, widely tipped to be the dominant player of the next decade, won her first Grand Slam title after a thrilling sudden death play-off with King.

At 21, Burton became not only the youngest winner of the du Maurier, but the youngest winner in women's major championship history.

First staged in 1973, the du Maurier did not receive its major status until 1979. Played each year on a prestigious Canadian course, this year the du Maurier will be held for the first time at the Ottawa Hunt Club, Ottawa, Ontario.

LPGA Tour Schedule 1994

FEBRUARY

4-6 Healthsouth Palm Beach Classic, Wycliffe Golf & Country Club, Lake Worth, Florida

17-19 Hawaiian Ladies Open, Ko Olina Golf Club, Ewa Beach, Oahu, Haw.

MARCH

2-5 Chrysler-Plymouth Tournament of Champions, Grand Cypress Resort, Orlando, Florida

10-13 Ping/Welch's Championship, Randolph Park North Golf Course, Tucson, Arizona

17-20 Standard Register Ping, Moon Valley, Phoenix, Arizona

24-27 *Nabisco Dinah Shore, Mission Hills Country Club, Rancho Mirage, Cal.

APRIL

15-17 Atlanta Women's Championship, Eagle's Landing Country Club, Stockbridge, Georgia

28-1 May Sprint Championship, Indigo Lakes Golf & Tennis Resort, Daytona Beach, Florida

MAY

6-8 Sara Lee Classic, Hermitage Golf Course, Old Hickory, Tennessee

12-15 *McDonald's LPGA Championship, Du Pont CC, Wilmington, Delaware

20-22 Lady Keystone Open, Hershey Country Club, Hershey, Pennsylvania

26-29 LPGA Corning Classic, Corning Country Club, Corning, New York

28-29 JC Penney/LPGA Skins Game, Stonebriar Country Club, Frisco, Tex.

JUNE

2-5 Oldsmobile Classic, Walnut Hills Country Club, East Lansing, Mich.

10-12 Minnesota LPGA Classic, Edinburgh USA Golf Course, Brooklyn Park, Minnesota

16-19 Rochester International, Locust Hill Country Club, Pittsford, New York

24-26 ShopRite LPGA Classic, Great Bay Resort & Country Club, Somers Point, New Jersey

JULY

1-3 Youngstown-Warren LPGA Classic, Avalon Lakes Golf Course, Warren, Ohio

8-10 Jamie Farr Toledo Classic, Highland Meadows Golf Club, Sylvania, Ohio

14-17 JAL Big Apple Classic, Wykagyl Country Club, New Rochelle, NY

21-24 *US Women's Open, Indianwood Golf Club, Lake Orion, Michigan

28-31 Ping/Welch's Championship, Blue Hill Country Club, Canton, Mass.

AUGUST

4-7 McCall's LPGA Classic at Stratton Mountain, Stratton Mountain Country Club, Stratton Mountain, Vermont

11-14 *Weetabix Women's British Open, Woburn G & CC, England

12-14 Dayton LPGA Classic, Country Club of the North, Dayton, Ohio

18-21 Chicago Challenge, White Eagle Golf Club, Naperville, Illinois

25-28 *du Maurier Ltd Classic, Ottawa Hunt Club, Ottawa, Ontario, Canada

SEPTEMBER

3-5 State Farm Rail Classic, Rail Golf Club, Springfield, Illinois

9-11 Ping-Cellular One Championship, Columbia Edgewater Country Club, Portland, Oregon

15-18 Safeco Classic, Meridian Valley Country Club, Kent, Washington

22-25 TBA

29-2 Oct Heartland Classic, Forest Hills Country Club, St Louis, Missouri

OCTOBER

13-16 World Championship of Women's Golf, venue TBA

21-23 Solheim Cup, The Greenbrier, White Sulphur Springs, W. Virginia

28-30 Nichirei International, Ami Golf Club, Ibaragi-Ken, Japan

NOVEMBER

4-6 Toray Japan Queens Cup, TBA

DECEMBER

1-4 JCPenney Classic Innisbrook Resort, Tarpon Springs, Florida

*Major Championship • TBA: To Be Arranged

WPG European Tour Schedule 1994

APRIL

21-24   Ford Golf Classic, Woburn G & CC (Duchess Course), Milton Keynes, England

MAY

19-22   Ladies' Open Costa Azul, Montado, Troia and Aroeira GC, Lisbon, Portugal

JUNE

9-12   Evian Masters, Royal Golf Club Evian, France

16-19   OVB Damen Open in Austria, GC Europa-Sportregion Zell am See/Kaprun, Nr Salzburg, Austria

23-26   BMW European Masters, Golf du Bercuit, Nr Brussels, Belgium

30-3   Hennessy Ladies' Cup, Golf und Landclub Koln, Germany

JULY

7-10   European Ladies' Golf Classic, TBA, Germany

28-31   Ford Irish Open, TBA, Ireland

AUGUST

4-7   Scottish Open, Dalmahoy Hotel G & CC, Edinburgh, Scotland

11-14   Weetabix Women's British Open, Woburn G & CC (Dukes Course), Milton Keynes, England

18-21   Trygg Hansa Ladies' Open, Haninge GC, Nr Stockholm, Sweden

SEPT

1-4   Ladies' English Open, The Tytherington Club, Nr Manchester, England

9-11   Netherlands Ladies' Open, Rijk van Nijmegen, Groesbeek, Netherlands

22-25   BMW Italian Ladies' Open. Lignano GC, Nr Venice, Italy

29-2 Oct   La Manga Club Spanish Open, La Mange Club, Cartagena, Spain

OCTOBER

12-15   Var Open de France Feminin, TBA, France

· MAJOR AMATEUR DATES FOR 1994 ·

JUNE

7-11   British Women's Amateur Championship, Newport GC, Rogerstone, Newport, Gwent, Wales

JULY

21-24   US Women's Amateur Championship, The Homestead, Hot Springs, Virginia

30-31   The Curtis Cup, The Honors Course, Chattanooga, Tennessee

SEPT

28-1   World Amateur Team Championship, The National GC, Paris, France

The Curtis Cup

The Curtis Cup

An Introduction

Two years on and the question remains the same: how do you follow Hoylake? Of the 27 Curtis Cup encounters that preceded 1992's installment at Royal Liverpool (or Hoylake as it is better known) it is hard to imagine that any could have exceeded the quality of this one. It had everything: a famous venue, a wonderful atmosphere and a dramatic conclusion.

Great Britain and Ireland will doubtless have fonder memories of Hoylake as it was they who achieved a famous victory on the final green of the final match. In recent years amateur teams from the Old World have had considerable cause for celebration with Great Britain and Ireland winning on three of the last four occasions; however, a quick glance at the full Roll of Honour reveals that teams from the New World have done rather better in times past.

The Honors Course at Chattanooga is the venue for the 1994 match. Elizabeth Boatman will again captain Great Britain and Ireland and the United States will be led by Lancy Smith. As for the course, it may not have the history and tradition of a Hoylake but it is an extremely fine test of golf and is certain to be beautifully presented. Let us hope that in two years time we are all wondering, 'How do you graduate after The Honors?'

Victorious at Hoylake (below) GB & Ireland will defend the Curtis Cup at the Honors Course, Chattanooga (opposite) at the end of July (30 - 31)

· ROLL OF HONOUR ·

YEAR	VENUE	WINNERS	SCORE
1932	Wentworth, England	USA	5½ - 3½
1934	Chevy Chase, USA	USA	6½ - 2½
1936	Gleneagles, Scotland	Tied	4½ - 4½
1938	Essex, USA	USA	5½ - 3½
1948	Royal Birkdale, England	USA	6½ - 2½
1950	Buffalo, USA	USA	7½ - 1½
1952	Muirfield, Scotland	GB&I	5 - 4
1954	Merion, USA	USA	6 - 3
1956	Prince's, England	GB&I	5 - 4
1958	Brae Burn, USA	Tied	4½ - 4½
1960	Lindrick, England	USA	6½ - 2½
1962	Broadmoor, USA	USA	8 - 1
1964	Royal Porthcawl, Wales	USA	10½ - 7½
1966	Cascades, USA	USA	13 - 5
1968	Royal County Down, NI	USA	10½ - 7½
1970	Brae Burn, USA	USA	11½ - 6½
1972	Western Gailes, Scotland	USA	10 - 8
1974	San Francisco, USA	USA	13 - 5
1976	Royal Lytham, England	USA	11½ - 6½
1978	Apawamis, USA	USA	12 - 6
1980	St Pierre, Wales	USA	13 - 5
1982	Denver, USA	USA	14½ - 3½
1984	Muirfield, Scotland	USA	9½ - 8½
1986	Prairie Dunes, USA	GB&I	13 - 5
1988	Royal St Georges, England	GB&I	11 - 7
1990	Somerset Hills, USA	USA	14 - 4
1992	Royal Liverpool, England	GB&I	10 - 8

P i n g   W o m e n ' s   G o l f   Y e a r

The 28th Curtis Cup

30 - 31 JULY • THE HONORS COURSE, CHATTANOOGA, TENNESSEE

A Preview by Lewine Mair

One legacy of all the hammerings Great Britain and Ireland have taken over the years in the Curtis Cup is that there are those in Britain who are even now inclined to worry less about winning the contest than making a match of it.

The British wins of 1986 and 1988 did much to allay such anxieties but when, in 1990, the Great Britain and Ireland team were comprehensively beaten at Somerset Hills, there was the unpalatable thought that they had

1992 revisited: the final moments of a memorable contest

perhaps slipped back into their old losing ways. The Americans had for years been seen as the stronger putting nation and, on the swift and slippery surfaces in New Jersey, they had putted the visitors off the greens.

Thus it was that coach loads of spectators – they came from the length and breadth of Britain – poured into Hoylake for the 1992 instalment with their fingers crossed. As it turned out, they need not have worried. The GB and Ireland side got off on the right foot and, to borrow the words used by the legendary Joyce Heathcoat Amory when, as

Joyce Wethered, she defeated America's equally legendary Glenna Collett in the final of the 1929 British Championship at St Andrews, 'the match was everything a good match ought to be'.

In the end, as many will no doubt recall, it all came down to the last hole of the last single. The links was glittering in the afternoon sun, crowds lined the fairway and, to add to the occasion, the denouement was being watched by His Royal Highness Prince Andrew, whose handicap, as I write, is on the verge of dipping into single figures.

The cast in the closing scene consisted of Vicki Goetze, 19 years of age and a former US Amateur champion, and Caroline Hall, 18 years of age and a winner of the English Girls' championship who had gone on to win the English Women's title. Goetze, a student of the University of Georgia at the time, was seen as the best all round amateur of her era. She was not a long hitter but she was – and still is, for that matter – as accurate with her four wood as many others are with an eight iron.

Hall was no less admiring of Goetze's ability than the next person but, as she stood on Hoylake's 18th tee, she thought of her own strengths. This daughter of an assistant headmaster knew she was the longer hitter and that Hoylake's final hole was one where length, perhaps as much as anything else, was a factor.

Actually, there was not too much difference in the drives, although it was Goetze who had to hit first towards the brightly ringed green. It was one of those rare occasions, and one which will doubtless haunt her till the end of her golfing days, when her four wood let her down. Instead of nestling by the flag, her ball subsided into the right hand greenside bunker.

Now everything depended on Hall and there was not a soul among the supporting hordes who did not have heart in mouth as the Bristol girl, her blonde hair reflecting the sun, stood over her four iron.

What was going on in her head?

'I was thinking to myself, it's now or never', she confided, later.

She kept her head still and hit. The silence was broken by a rising roar from the greenside crowd as the ball touched down just ten feet from the flag. With a still shaken Goetze taking three to get down from sand, Hall made her winning four.

It amounted to a thrilling occasion for the home players and supporters. Not just because of the victory but because the match had been close and the golf from both teams better than anyone could ever remember.

Both the Americans and British will tell you that their respective professional circuits have made a difference to the level of the amateur game. Where once the players were understandably reluctant to give their all to an amateur game which, in career terms, led nowhere, they have over the years come to see golf as a career. And the Curtis Cup as the best possible qualification to take with them into that arena.

JoAnne Carner, who will be captaining this year's US Solheim Cup side at The Greenbrier in October, believes that the improvement in the British owes most to better and more uniform teaching. 'In my Curtis Cup days,' she drawled, 'the British and the Irish girls were fine competitors who simply did not have what it takes technically. They were up on their toes at the top of the backswing.'

Belle Robertson, who represented GB and Ireland in the winning team of 1986, at a time when she was over 50, agreed with

Carner's suggestion but, at the same time, put forward her own theory that the British have benefited enormously from infiltrating the American University system.

Chattanooga bound: Scotland's Catriona Lambert is likely to be a key member of the GB & Ireland team

She explained how Karen Davies' presence in the team of '86 had made all the difference. The Welsh player, who had been at university in Florida (winning several open college titles) had seen the Americans on good days and bad.

When, at the match, sister members of the British team began to quake at the mere mention of the Americans' golfing credentials, Davies was able to bring up some occasion in a college event when she had witnessed the same players make a perfect hash of things. 'What Karen did', said Robertson, 'was to convince the rest of us that the Americans were not invincible. They were no different from anyone else.'

Things have moved on since 1992 and that memorable last afternoon at Hoylake. Both Hall and Goetze, for example, were among those to turn professional following that clash, thereby making way for a series of new players to take aim on the 1994 edition of a match which, hardened professionals such as Louise Suggs and the aforementioned Carner, still see as the pinnacle of their golfing careers. (Suggs, incidentally, was not too long ago recalling the match of 1948 which took place after a ten year gap. So moved were the visiting Americans by the state of post war Britain in general and the fact that the British golfers were having to make do with rickety, old fashioned equipment, that several handed their clubs to their opponents before taking the boat home.)

The British selectors have been fortunate in that they were able to use the 1993 Vagliano Trophy match at Morfontaine in September as a preliminary test for their Curtis Cup squad.

The players who made up the wining GB and Ireland team on that occasion were as follows: Catriona Lambert, the 1993 British Amateur champion; Julie Hall, who was named (jointly) with Lambert as the Daily Telegraph's golfer of the year; Lisa Walton, Janice Moodie, Kirsty Speak, Joanne Morley, Nicola Buxton, Mhairi McKay and Joanne Hockley.

Since then, Morley, another star turn at Hoylake, has switched to the professional ranks, but that is not to say that the remaining eight will necessarily slip into the Curtis Cup octet which will tee up at Chattanooga on July 30th. They will need to demonstrate their form at the start of the 1994 season.

The Americans, for their part, will have

Thomas is not only ineligible but she'll be playing for the opposition.'

Thomas, of course, is that celebrated little Welsh golfer who, later this season, should play for the Principality for a twenty-fourth consecutive occasion in the women's Home Internationals. Moreover, just as this

The blending of youth and experience: Vicki Goetze and Anne Sander formed a formidable partnership at Somerset Hills

come under scrutiny on their Orange Blossom Tour, a series of early season amateur events in Florida which, for the last few years, has attracted leading amateurs from around the golfing globe.

In which connection, it is not too many years since one Vicki Thomas had an excellent run on this particular beat, recording a sequence of impressive results in her month abroad.

When it was over and the American selectors met to discuss which of their players was shaping for a Curtis Cup place, one among the officials, leafing through the results, noted, 'This Vicki Thomas looks like the kind of player we need.'

'Well', returned another member of the US Committee, 'we can't have her!'

The lady across the table sat open mouthed before the other explained, 'Vicki

article was about to be fed into a fax machine, news came of how she had won a tournament – the South Atlantic – on this year's Orange Blossom circuit. You can be sure then that her name will be raised when the Curtis Cup selectors are finalising their optimum eight.

Meanwhile, when it comes to the American selectors' deliberations, it is fun to consider what they might say about Anne Sander, 52 years of age when she played in the winning team of 1990, and still going strong. Last year, she won her fourth American senior title. Foursomes are Sander's forte and, should her captain pair her with a Jill McGill or a Sarah Ingram, she would unsettle many a younger foe.

Nothing is certain – only that both sides are on the right track for their Chattanooga destination.

The Solheim Cup

The Solheim Cup

An Introduction

Tempus fugit. Time flies, as the old Latin saying goes, and for most of us the 1980s are still fairly fresh in the memory. So how come it is so difficult to remember life before the Solheim Cup? Before 1990 there was no biennial contest between the women professionals of the United States and their counterparts from Europe. But where would they (and we for that matter) be without it now?

The question is perhaps most pertinent to the members of the European team who triumphed at Dalmahoy in 1992; their success has totally transformed the perception of women's golf in Europe, and

The class of 1990: the US won the inaugural contest at Lake Nona

to hear some of the players talk, the Solheim Cup appears almost to be their raison d'être, as the old French saying goes.

So there have been only two matches: Lake Nona, Florida in 1990 and Dalmahoy, Scotland in 1992, and the series score stands at one win apiece.

Kathy Whitworth led the United States to an 11½ – 4½ win at Lake Nona and her team of eight comprised (from left to right in the picture opposite): Pat Bradley, Patty Sheehan, Nancy Lopez, Dottie Mochrie, Cathy Gerring, Betsy King, Rosie Jones and Beth Daniel. An inspired Daniel won maximum points from her three matches.

Two years later, and the number of players per side having been increased to ten, it was Mickey Walker's Europeans who were proudly parading the magnificent Waterford Crystal trophy following their

11½ – 6½ success. Her team members were (as above): Helen Alfredsson, Trish Johnson, Catrin Nilsmark, Laura Davies, Kitrina Douglas, Liselotte Neumann, Florence Descampe, Pam Wright, Alison Nicholas and Dale Reid. Davies gained three points from her three games and none of the three Swedish players was defeated – Alfredsson and Neumann each won two and a half points and Nilsmark made a remarkable debut by winning her only match and at the same time secured the winning point.

The Greenbrier, White Sulphur Springs, West Virginia is the venue for the 3rd Solheim Cup match. We have no crystal ball to tell us what will happen, but as to who might play and what *could* happen, read on...

The class of 1992: Europe levelled the series with a stunning victory at Dalmahoy

The 3rd Solheim Cup
The European Perspective

A Preview by Bill Johnson

Mickey Walker has had The Greenbrier on her mind since proudly holding aloft the Solheim Cup following Europe's staggering triumph at Dalmahoy two years ago.

After the inaugural encounter at Lake Nona in 1990, when the United States completed a comprehensive 11½ – 4½ victory, few gave Europe any realistic chance of winning two years later in Scotland, but then strange things can happen in golf. Even after Europe turned the tables with their 11½ – 6½ success at Dalmahoy, not everyone was convinced that this would act as the catalyst which would see the emergence of European players on the world stage.

'I think Trish Johnson explained the situation accurately when she cited the Solheim Cup victory as a turning point', says Walker, who will again captain the European team at The Greenbrier. 'It is all a question of confidence. The level of talent amongst the players is very similar but the difference is the confidence factor.'

'It has been noticeable with those who played at Dalmahoy but it has also been rubbing off on other players on the Tour who have raised their standards. These are the girls who have played alongside Laura Davies and other members of the European side. They thought that on their day they could beat the world's top players. Now they know that they can and they are proving themselves on a European Tour which is getting stronger all the time.'

America is the finishing school for golfers with ambitions of scaling the heights of their profession. It was the 'go west young man'

Unless her form dips dramatically, Annika Sorenstam will be heading for The Greenbrier

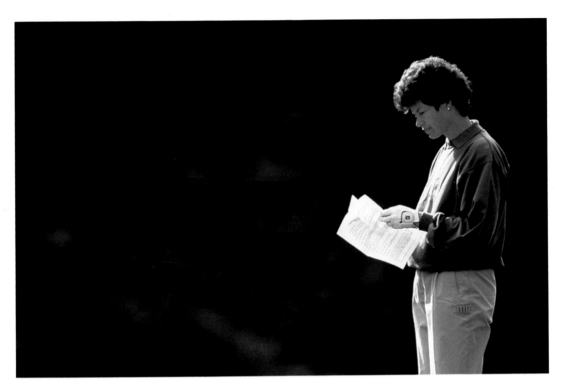

mentality which played such an important role in the careers of Nick Faldo, Seve Ballesteros, Sandy Lyle, Bernhard Langer and Ian Woosnam. It has been the same route which has paid dividends for the likes of Davies, Johnson, Lotta Neumann and Helen Alfredsson.

Alfredsson won the Nabisco Dinah Shore last year and this was quickly followed by Johnson's back-to-back victories in Las Vegas and Atlanta. Davies won the McDonald's Championship then Helen Dobson celebrated her brilliant rookie year by winning the State Farm Rail Classic.

At the end of the season, Davies, Alfredsson and Johnson had climbed into the top ten on the Ping Leaderboard while Suzanne Strudwick became the LPGA's 'Rookie of the Year'.

'They were marvellous performances and I would class Helen Dobson's play-off win

against Dottie Mochrie in her first year on the LPGA Tour as second only to Laura Davies winning the US Open championship,' suggests Walker.

Rehearsing her victory speech?! Europe's Captain, Mickey Walker

With a stronger European Tour taking shape under the direction of Terry Coates, and the support of the top players who divide their time on both sides of the Atlantic, more players are making the move into the professional ranks.

Already they are making an impact and Davies has no hesitation in saying, 'If anything, I think we will have a stronger team this year than we had at Dalmahoy. Some of these new girls on the Tour are already showing their paces and pushing the top players who will clearly have to fight to make the side.'

Each team for The Greenbrier will comprise ten players and in Europe's case five of these places will be earned automatically from the Solheim Cup standings list with Mickey Walker naming the remaining five members of her side.

While this differs from the manner in which the US team will be selected it is necessary because the European Tour's playing schedule has only half the number of tournaments on the LPGA Tour. With so many Europeans now playing on both tours their immediate problem could be fitting enough European events into their schedule to ensure an automatic place.

There is also a change in the format this year in that all ten members of the teams will play in each of the three series of games – an alteration that has not been welcomed by the European players.

The suggestion came from the LPGA whose viewpoint was that it was unfair for two players on each side to sit out the opening two series. It was something most American players had never encountered in representative games other than the Curtis Cup. Conversely, the Europeans had been brought up playing international matches where part of the captain's responsibility is to manoeuvre players strategically. There are cases for both arguments.

Meanwhile there is an intriguing season ahead as the Europeans continue their challenge for a place in Mickey Walker's team. There will be disappointments and moments for celebration as the 1994 season unfolds.

At the end of 1993 Annika Sorenstam from Sweden led the Solheim Cup standings followed by Laura Davies, Marie-Laure de Lorenzi from France, England's Lora Fairclough and Italian golfer Federica Dassu. They were the five leading the hunt for automatic places.

They were being chased by Alison Nicholas, Dale Reid, Helen Dobson, Catrin Nilsmark and Trish Johnson. The leading ten players included only five members from Europe's triumphant team at Dalmahoy.

Lotta Neumann was placed 11th, Pam Wright 16th and Helen Alfredsson 20th.

Belgian Florence Descampe needs a good year if she is to retain her place in the side

Belgium's Florence Descampe, who played in only three European events last year was 33rd while Kitrina Douglas, suffering from a loss of form was languishing in a lowly 49th position. They are the remaining members of the Dalmahoy side.

By far the greatest impression has been made by Sorenstam. The Stockholm golfer was NCAA champion while at the University of Arizona in 1991. She also won seven tournaments and was the losing finalist in the 1992 US Amateur. Last year, her first as a professional, she came fourth in the Standard Register Ping tournament in Phoenix and earned a top-10 finish in the Las Vegas LPGA at Canyon Gate before launching her European campaign. And what a campaign it was! Sorenstam finished second in four of the nine tournaments she

Open in Sweden, and Spain's Amaya Arruti in only her sixth outing as a professional won the Italian Open to join Fairclough and Helen Dobson as first-time winners.

'These performances underline the fact that we are developing a greater depth of talent and there is also Suzanne Strudwick of

Still to make her debut in the Solheim Cup, Suzanne Strudwick was last year's LPGA Rookie of the Year

entered in Europe to take the 'Rookie of the Year' award comfortably.

Marie-Laure de Lorenzi holds the European Tour record with seven victories in 1988, the first of two consecutive years during which she topped the Order of Merit. The Barcelona-based French golfer played at Lake Nona in the first Solheim Cup match since when she has worked on changes to her swing. In 1993 she was back to her best. She won her second French Open crown in the final tournament of the season to earn fourth place on the merit table. 'It is great to see Marie-Laure back,' says Walker. 'She is a great team member and a genuinely world-class player.'

Lora Fairclough held off one of the strongest fields of the season to seal a maiden victory when she won the IBM

course who came so close to a place in the Dalmahoy team. Winning the LPGA's Rookie of the Year title was another important step forward for her,' reasons the European captain.

But there will be no complacency at The Greenbrier. 'We will be going out to America as the underdogs this time, especially after winning at Dalmahoy. The Americans will be very determined to regain the Solheim Cup and I have enormous respect and admiration for JoAnne Carner who will captain their team.'

'We played together when I was on the LPGA Tour. I think she will inspire her players and prove to be a great choice as captain. Whoever wins in October I am sure that the 1994 Solheim Cup will be a marvellous and memorable occasion.'

The 3rd Solheim Cup
The US Perspective

A Preview by Dick Taylor

Sorry, European supporters of women's golf, the Colonies are going to wrest the Solheim Cup away from your talented 10 who stunned the world two years ago at Dalmahoy.

Given the same cast of two years ago, the outcome in October this year will be reversed for one reason – or person.... team captain JoAnne Gunderson Carner. The maiden name is used in order to identify her early career when she was the Great Gundy, five-time winner of the US Women's Amateur, as well as a myriad other match-play events and was 6-3-1 in Curtis Cup play, taking no prisoners once in the lead.

She was the consummate match-play golfer of her considerable era. Foes would admit they felt two down at the first tee,

facing off against the seemingly ever-so-pleasant strawberry blonde with the Nordic ice-blue eyes. It was those eyes that betrayed her, once the game was on. They became laser-blue, and the smile became grim. This kid hated to lose.

Mrs Carner mellowed – a little – as her professional career became as incandescent as her amateur career. Either is worthy of Hall of Fame inclusion. Included in her 41 victories as an LPGA member are two US Opens, and, with a US Junior win on her dossier, she has eight national titles. And nearly $3 million in earnings.

At age 55 she should be enjoying the fruits of her labour, which include a deep-sea fishing boat, docked near Don and JoAnne Carners' oceanfront Palm Beach double condominium and a mountain cabin

If anyone can inspire a group of players it is JoAnne Carner – Hall of Fame member – and Captain of the US team at The Greenbrier

in Tennessee for trout fishing. However, golf *is* her recreation; you can tell by her zest on course. Besides, the tour is her second home, and she knows very well she can win again and become the oldest warrior to ever win a regular tour event, male or female. If she would get off the right leg

championships; eight are millionaires (three having won over $4million).

If you are thinking prima donna problems, forget it. Only the captain of this cruise has the right to that appellation. Even Nancy Lopez, a mature mom with 47 victories and a few strokes away from

more often and not consider putting a geometric science, she will win again.

Put all her facets together: match-play terror, continuing pride in her game, her place in history, and you just know she is not about to be captain of the first American Solheim Cup side to lose on home soil. No way!

Just what do you suppose this great motivator (she has picked many a youngster up off the floor and gotten them on the tee again) will do with her projected team of 10? They own the best part of 150 titles between them, including 18 major

$4 million in earnings, will have to listen to the advice of this sagacious campaigner. Her likely line-up will come from this array of stars: Lopez; Betsy King, arguably the greatest player of the past decade; latest sensation Brandie Burton; tenacious Dottie Mochrie; new Hall of Famer Patty Sheehan; Lauri Merten, a late bloomer; Meg Mallon; Donna Andrews, a bigcourse player; Sherri Steinhauer and Captain Carner may choose to introduce another newcomer from the likes of Tammie Green, Michelle McGann,

Rising star, Donna Andrews is challenging strongly for a place among the 'elite ten'

Dana Lofland-Dormann, or alternatively, opt for even more experience by selecting Pat Bradley or Beth Daniel. Juli Inkster is on maternity leave.

It will be no surprise if Tammie Green is selected The Europeans have shown amazing growth since the first Solheim Cup in

Orlando, Florida, losing 11½ to 4½. Back then the star-struck members of the WPG European Tour were asking for autographs from American counterparts. Two years later the pendulum had swung the other way, but no one knew it until it was too late, from America's standpoint.

Clearly Europe's finest were the best of the week. They also had the advantage of weather. Americans, pros and amateurs alike, stay close to the hearth when such weather as experienced at Dalmahoy sets in. And there was slight disarray when captain Kathy Whitworth was called home by her mother's death.

Captain Mickey Walker, a certain positive factor in the Euro team's makeup, knows that Lopez's absence in Scotland, with her depth of experience and 'fear factor' presence, is a likely hurdle this time out. But her charges two years ago, from the outset, displayed an aggressiveness and poise that rattled the visitors.

This infant international match by-passed the crawling stage required of new additions to the scene, thanks largely to Europe's victory. It didn't take decades to make everyone sit up and take notice, à la the Ryder Cup. Another factor is the sponsor, Karsten Manufacturing, with the gracious hosts, Louise and Karsten Solheim, adding rock-solid backing.

This will be the third playing and all three have been blessed by superior venues. Lake Nona in Orlando is among the most respected of modern facilities in the United States, Dalmahoy, site of the second match near Edinburgh, is a charming golf mecca in the Scottish mould; that is, historic, famous and perfectly run.

And now comes the The Greenbrier, in quaint White Sulphur Springs, West Virginia. If there were such things as six stars given to resorts, this would be the only one on the planet to earn such an accolade. From the moment you are greeted at the stately, columned, entrance, until you depart pounds heavier and every day woes far lighter, you are in a cocoon called service, or Southern hospitality.

For openers, if Hollywood had been aware, 'Gone With the Wind' could have filmed interiors at The Greenbrier. Sweeping staircases, opulent decor, cabins for slave quarters, and an overwhelming, but tasteful facade of part White House, Augusta National, Jefferson Memorial housing a great spa, great kitchen, and accommodations. Fiddley-dee-dee, isn't that Scarlett buying bon bons at the chocolate shop?

The rich and famous and as wealth spread, not so famous, have been coming to this queen among last bastions of gentility since 1778. They came for the springs and to be pampered. Lately they come for golf and tennis and to see the ninth wonder of the world, resident legend Sam Snead. The horsey set thinks The Greenbrier was invented for them, but golf has been the mainstay since the turn of the century.

Although the game first came to the Shenandoah Valley in 1884 – the nearby six-hole Oakhurst Links being the first organised club on the continent – the origins of the present day Greenbrier course can be traced to 1924, when it was laid out by the pioneering golf architect, Charles Blair McDonald; it has been used for competitions ever since. In 1977 Jack Nicklaus modernised the course for Ryder Cup play in 1979 and it now runs 6,721 yards from the medal tees. From 1985-1987 the Senior PGA Tour scheduled a stop at the old resort, and it was a homecoming for those veterans who had competed in the Greenbrier Open in the 1950s.

Surrounded by the Allegheny Mountains, and with dramatic elevation changes, The Greenbrier course is one of the most beautiful of inland, park-type courses in America. In the autumn, changing colour in the leaves will only accentuate this beauty.

No matter what the outcome of the match might be, all visitors will have experienced a slice of Americana. Once the setting for Southern belles and balls, warm hospitality and exquisite amenities, only the belles are missing these

The Greenbrier possesses tradition, challenge and charm

days in an era when gracious, languid living seems to be vanishing.

And if the cuisine does become a little overwhelming by week's end, then on the way to the airport one can stop off in downtown White Sulphur Springs and get a burger and fries as the first step back into reality.